SWEET & SNAPPY
CHERRY DRINKS

SWEET & SNAPPY
CHERRY DRINKS

The Ultimate Guide to Cherry Cocktails and Non-Alcoholic Beverages

Lori Hall Steele

With a Foreword by Russel Reiter, Ph.D.

EIGHTH SEA BOOKS
TRAVERSE CITY, MICHIGAN

Eighth Sea Books, P.O. Box 1925
Traverse City, MI 49684
info@8thseabooks.com
www.8thseabooks.com

Visit our Web site: www.cherrydrinks.com

Printed in the United States of America

Library of Congress Control Number: 2004092915
Print ed. ISBN: 0-9749549-0-X
PDF ed. ISBN: 0-9749549-1-8

Publisher's Cataloging in Publication Data
Steele, Lori Hall.
    Sweet & snappy cherry drinks : the ultimate guide to cherry cocktails and
non-alcoholic beverages / Lori Hall Steele. -- 1st ed. Traverse City, Mich. :
Eighth Sea Books, 2004
        p. ; cm.
        Includes index.
        ISBN: 0-9749549-0-X
        1. Beverages. 2. Cookery (Cherries) 3. Cocktails. 4. Nonalcoholic
cocktails. 5. Cherry--Nutritional aspects. I. Title. II. Sweet and snappy
cherry drinks

TX815 .S74 2004   2004092915
641.2--dc22   0406

For my son,

Jackson Gabriel Steele.

May he always experience

the same northern springtimes

as his greats and great-greats:

A magical world

dressed in the first white

of cherry blossoms.

CONTENTS

FOREWORD

Tart cherry products, besides providing "sweet and snappy" tastes to drinks or foodstuffs, are remarkably healthy. Research on the ingredients in tart cherries at Michigan State University and the University of Texas Health Science Center over the last decade has revealed that they contain a variety of highly effective antioxidants. Dietary antioxidants are important because their consumption helps the body defend itself from damage due to highly toxic molecules produced in cells; these toxic agents are referred to as free radicals. Besides the conventional, well-known agent, vitamin C, tart cherries contain an abundance of other antioxidants including anthocyanins and the newly discovered free radical scavenger, melatonin. Anthocyanins not only provide tart cherries with their pleasing crimson hue, but they also support the body's fight against diseases that involve free radicals. Likewise, melatonin, which was only recently found to exist in plants, is in high quantities in tart cherries and it is an efficient antioxidant.

Anthocyanins and melatonin work individually and synergistically to reduce the ravages of aging and a variety of free radical-based diseases. These antioxidants are not only present in fresh and frozen tart cherries, but they are likewise preserved in processed cherry concoctions—for example, dried cherry powder, cherry juice concentrate, cherry pie filling, and others. The consumption of any tart cherry product is followed by the uptake of the antioxidants into the body where they ward off tissue destruction (referred to scientifically as oxidative stress) that is a consequence of aging and disease. Oxidative stress is the total amount of molecular debris that cells of any individual gradually accumulates throughout a lifetime.

The inclusion of tart cherry products into a healthful diet

may assist in forestalling disease processes related to oxidative stress and/or reduce the severity of free radical damage to tissues of the body. In this book, Lori Hall Steele provides a gamut of drink recipes that make the consistent use of cherry products not only highly palatable, but these easily prepared drinks may additionally benefit your physical well-being.

Russel J. Reiter, Ph.D.
University of Texas Health Science Center
Author of *Melatonin*

INTRODUCTION

After Michigan State University revealed that tart cherries contain seventeen pain-relieving, health-benefiting antioxidants, *Newsweek* asked "'Take ten cherries and call me in the morning?' The day doctors say that may not be far off." Indeed, cherries are healthy—how can you go wrong with more than seventeen vitamins, minerals and other compounds that scavenge free radicals, fight disease and repair cells? No wonder word-of-mouth has launched an underground health craze.

The big surprise in creating this book is not how healthy cherries are. It is, rather, just how great-tasting, adaptable—and fun—cherry drinks can be. These 204 recipes extol the many moods of this classic fruit: its bright, springtime essence in saketinis (the new cosmo), its dusky warmth in cider blends, its glamorous effervescence in champagne cocktails. Recipes range from adaptations of timeless classics (Shirley Temples, cherry Coke, Manhattans, mojitos) to brand-new drinks created just for these pages.

Concentrate, a thick liquid, also can make for some playful and pretty drinks. The Lava Lamp, for instance, features thick red concentrate dripping down ice cubes into a bubbly, clear vodka mix. Concentrate can create special effects: Pop-art circles in the bottom of a flute, a scarlet wash coating a goblet's interior. The crimson color makes for bold mixes in general, and especially for holidays (think Valentine's, Christmas, Halloween).

Cherry plays well with others. It mixes just as easily with orange juice and soda pop as with whiskey and wine. It can be substituted in nearly any drink that calls for grenadine. And, almost regardless of the type of drink, the taste works—cherry transforms from sweet innocence in children's spritzers to mod sexiness in atomic-age cocktails to old-school manliness in classic mixed drinks.

Real cherry juice may be as old as the trees, but it's a relative newcomer to U.S. grocery store shelves, and it's still not available everywhere. Yet.

After the antioxidant discovery, concentrate went from being a food additive (used largely for flavoring) to becoming somewhat of a health fad—consumers scattered across the nation became hooked on the ruby-red elixir, claiming it eased migraines, arthritis pain, and gout. Others declared it helped digestion. Still others said it was the only thing that helped them sleep through the night. Researchers said eight to twenty cherries a day, particularly Montmorency tarts, could ease inflammation and other ailments. One ounce of concentrate contains the juice of about fifty cherries.

Small companies began repackaging concentrate for consumers, and sales multiplied, 800 percent in 2001 and 2002 alone. Meanwhile, universities began studies to see if those antioxidants prevented certain cancers and slowed aging, research that's expected to continue for some time. A national food company has already proved tart cherries reduce pain and inflammation. Up here in northern Michigan—the nation's Cherry Capital, a charmed region where half the country's Montmorency tarts are grown—this was especially good news: A new hope for farmers and land preservation.

In all the hoopla, nobody really talked much about how cherry juice actually tasted. After I finally sampled some, I wondered why it wasn't a staple in households and behind every bar in America. Meanwhile, in some places, cherry concentrate was relegated to the pharmacy.

Despite the fabulous health benefits, these recipes demonstrate that cherries don't taste a bit like medicine. And forget the taste of almond-flavored maraschinos, which aren't even close. Forget, too, the taste of most cherry juices from grocery stores, which often are mixes of apple, grape and artificial flavorings.

Real cherry isn't like that. Real cherry tangs in your mouth. It hits with a slight sweetness and something close to sass. Though it rarely overpowers, it has a definite presence—its own very-cherry mojo. Cheers!

CHEER EASE
A HANGOVER AID?

A cocktail that's good for you? That was the big question after recipe contributors mentioned that the *really* good thing about these cocktails—beyond the taste, beyond the health benefits—was that when they consumed cherry drinks, they didn't get a hangover.

Too good to be true? That may be. Still, it seemed worth investigating. Could the natural magic of cherries help foil one of mankind's oldest curses? I was curious, so I tracked down a national alcohol expert. Dr. James Schaefer—a professor at Union College in Schenectady, New York, who *Omni* magazine called "The Indiana Jones of the Tavern Scene"—was skeptical about the cherry cure, but curious. Curious enough to graciously agree to shepherd a double-blind study for this book. And despite showing mixed results, cherry drinks did ease some volunteers' hangovers enough to indicate that further research is, indeed, warranted, in Dr. Schaefer's opinion, with more rigorous and refined testing.

Many will ask whether hangovers are worth investigating. They are, after all, the price of overindulgence. But consider that beyond the obvious personal pain—headache, fatigue, nausea—hangovers cost U.S. businesses more than $148 billion annually in absenteeism and poor performance. A more-recent survey showed that 48 percent of young professionals at leading British corporations worked with hangovers at least once a week. Other studies show that light and moderate drinkers are most likely to suffer hangovers, whereas some 60 percent of heavy drinkers never feel the pain.

Despite the prevalence of hangovers, the condition is not well understood scientifically. The characteristics, however, are well known, and include dehydration, headache, nausea and fatigue. Though cherries and hangovers have not been studied, Dr. Russel Reiter, the nation's leading melatonin expert (see *Foreword*), said it is "conceivable" that cherries could mitigate hangover symptoms.

Here's why, potentially: The antioxidants in cherries synergize to create a natural anti-inflammatory painkiller that some claim is ten times more effective than aspirin (researchers suggest eight to twenty cherries a day for pain, and one ounce of concentrate contains fifty cherries). Many folks also swear by cherries to ease indigestion and related stomach woes. Alcohol depletes melatonin, which regulates sleep. Since cherries contain more melatonin than any other natural food, replenishing it while drinking theoretically could enable a deeper state of sleep, preventing fatigue that typically accompanies a hangover. Additionally, nutrients in cherries may replenish those depleted as alcohol is metabolized. This is, of course, only theoretical.

This book's double-blind study on cherry drinks included nineteen volunteers ranging in age from 24 to 67, including light to heavy drinkers who average two to ten drinks per occasion. Volunteers agreed to consume the same type and number of drinks on two consecutive Fridays at cocktail parties. One week, they drank cocktails containing cherry concentrate; the next week they consumed a placebo—grenadine, in this case—but were unaware of what they were consuming. Volunteers acted as their own controls, providing information on their typical drinking habits and average severity of twenty-five hangover symptoms, then rating themselves the morning after each cocktail party.

The results were mixed. Two volunteers dropped out due to illness and scheduling conflicts. Two simply never get hangovers. Two did not drink enough to provoke an average hangover. Three more consumed different amounts on each night, making comparisons difficult. One came down with a cold on the morning after. Despite the flaws, however, six volunteers reported feeling much better the morning after consuming cherry drinks.

Statistically, when Dr. Schaefer crunched the numbers (using the McNemar Test for Significant Changes), there was little overall evidence that cherries diminished hangovers. But there was enough anecdotal corroboration of the cherry-cure theory—those six people swear they felt better, in several cases *much* better, when they drank cherry drinks—that further study seems reasonable. Dr. Schaefer says there is room for repetition of the study with better controls, a larger sample, refinement of the topic, and recruitment of subjects who experience more severe hangovers.

My own gut feeling, based on the double-blind test as well as hearsay and experimentation with friends, is that cherries may work for some people, but that the biological basis will remain unclear until it's understood why some people experience hangovers while others simply don't. I also suspect that, for those people, cherries may allay some effects of moderate drinking—say, having a few margaritas to celebrate a coworker's birthday—much better than frat-house-style binges. It could be, too, that a proportion of cherry drinks—say, two of four drinks—is a more effective hangover-alleviating dose than drinking cherry cocktails all night.

Though cherries have been around forever, the concept of cherry drinks is relatively new, and the fact that some people claim hangovers are relieved by cherries is worth considering. I'm interested in hearing from those of you who may have experienced effects of cherries on hangovers, or from those of you who may have insights on the subject. If you'd like to share, simply go to this book's Web site, www.cherrydrinks.com.

Finally, some warnings: This study says that some people felt better the morning after drinking cherry cocktails, compared to the morning after drinking cocktails without cherries. This study does not suggest that cherries are a silver bullet or that cherry drinks can be overindulged in without consequence. I want to encourage responsible drinking: Please, enjoy cherry drinks, but do not harm yourself or others.

CHERRIES ON TOP: A BRIEF HISTORY

For Samurais—who were expected to give their lives in their prime—cherry blossoms symbolized the ideal military spirit: Something beautiful and pure blown down from the branches. Danes, meanwhile, believed forest demons lodged in cherry trees. Serbs believed beautiful and heartbreaking fairy-like creatures called Vila lived near cherry trees, where they danced and sang wearing only white.

Devil or angel? Who can say? The spirit of cherries in legend is as unfixed as its essence in drinks: one minute innocent; the next minute, on the edge of sinfulness.

Cherries date to at least 600 B.C., when Chinese noblemen dined on them and Persians traded the tart, ruby-red fruit. Its name derives from *cerasus* (now its Latin name) which comes from the Greek *kerasos*, a word thought to be taken from a very cherry-filled Turkish city on the Black Sea.

It likely did not take long for cherries to find their way into drinks, hard and soft. Cherry melomel is a fruity version of mead, a fermented honey drink that's the oldest known alcohol-containing drink. Korean Buddhist monks developed delicious hot teas made from fruits, including cherries. Russian czars sent their cooks to monasteries so they could perfect their honey-cooking skills for such drinks as Ancient Happy Cherry Honey, a mead-like beverage.

Cherries migrated as Europeans did, finding their way in the 1600s to U.S. colonies. Sweets and tarts spread up the Saint Lawrence Seaway to the Great Lakes where the water worked wonders, tempering Arctic winds in winter and subduing heat in summer. Cherries flourished. And so did cherry bounces—made by soaking fruit in liquor. Bounces were popular colonial-era drinks and continue to be made to this day with recipes passed from generation to generation. Meanwhile, French Creoles were making ratafia, soaking ripe cherries in alcohol for several days, then adding sugar syrup to encourage fermentation.

In the 1800s, commercial distilleries began producing such cherry liqueurs as kirschwasser, Cherry Heering and maraschino, a sweet cordial made from the fermented juice and crushed almond-flavored stones of Croatia's small, bitter, wild marasca cherry. Cherries soaked in this liqueur became a delicacy—the maraschino cherry (today they are flavored with almond).

Cherry liqueurs soon were part of such popular drinks as the Singapore Sling and potent Zombies. And the maraschino itself became an icon—the ubiquitous Cherry on Top. Are they innocent as an all-American soda shop sipper? Or worldly as a cherry splashing into a New York cocktail?

Either way, a new phase in the history of cherries has clearly begun. Now, the prospect of bettered health is pushing maraschinos aside and placing tart cherries on top. And people are just drinking it up.

DRINKS FOR ALL OCCASIONS

·ACADEMY AWARDS
Betty Paige 66
Lady Brett 103
Mary Pickford 86
Pink Mink Martini 75
Red Rhett Butler 96
Ruby Slippers 101
The Red Carpet 61

·AFTER DINNER
Cherry Bounce/Cordial 65
Cherry Bounce No. 3 65
Lady Brett 103
Red, Red Wine 62
Traverse Cherry Bounce 65

·BIRTHDAY PARTIES
Ballet Slippers 34
Cherry Fizz Punch 49

Cherry Sangria 50
Cherry Slush No. 2 51
Chocula-Cherry 36
Pretty in Pink 38
Radio Flyer 38
Red Light Stop! 39
Superpowered Ginger Blaster 39
Shirley Temple 40

·CHRISTMAS
Cherry-Vanilla TraVini 73
Cherry Bellini 58
Cherry Fizzle Punch 99
Cherry Wassail 53
Festive Cherry Punch 51
Mulled Cherry Wine 107
Ruby Slippers 101
Wassailing Cherries 88

·DERBY DAYS
Red Rhett Butler 96
Scarlet Julep 97

·EUROPEAN IMPORTS
Cafe Kirsch 67
Cherry Bellini 58
Cherry Nalivka 66
Cherry Sangria 50
Northern Lights Sangria 101
Pyramid Point Pimm's Cup 70
Snakebite Red 62

·FALL DRINKS
Candy Apple 94
Cherry Cider 35
Hot Spiced Cider 54
Mulled Cherry Wine 107
Mulled Cider 107
Red, Red Wine 62
Tart N' Stormy 88

·FATHER'S DAY
Betty Paige 66
Crimson Highball 95
Miss American Pie 96
Old Mission Manhattan 96
Red Eye 61
Scarlet Gimlet 81
Sweet & Sour 44
Traverse Cherry Bounce 65

·FLAMING DRINKS
Fiery Blue Blazer 105
Flaming Volcano 100
Northern Squall (Hurricane) 87

·FOURTH OF JULY
Cherry Fizzle Punch 99
Cherry Slush No. 1 50
Iced Cherry Sparkle Tea 52
Miss American Pie 96
Red, White & Blue 80
Red Fish, Blue Fish 80

·HALLOWEEN
Northern Gothic 103
Pink Witch 87
Red Nasty 62
Red Witch 62
Snakebite Red 62

·MARDI GRAS
Northern Squall (Hurricane) 87

·MORNING REVELRIES
Cairn Side Sunrise 67
Cherry-Pom Mimosa 59
Cherry Bellini 58
Crimson Mimosa 59
Northern Sunrise 92

·MOTHER'S DAY
Ballet Slippers 34
Cherry Bellini 58
Pink Mink Martini 75
Pink Slipper 61

·NEW YEAR'S EVE
Ballet Slippers 34
Festive Cherry Punch 51
Pink Mink Martini 75
Pink Slippers 61
Ruby Slippers 101

·RETRO
Betty Paige 66
Flaming Volcano 100
I Love Lucy 79
Lava Lamp 79

·SOUTH OF BORDER
Aurora Caipirinha 83
Cherryrita 90
Cherry Cuba Libre 84
Cherry Mojito 85
Margarita Party 100
Northern Frostbite 92
Scarlet Sangria 102

27

·SPRING DRINKS
Pink Cherry Blosson 60
Pink Geisha Saketini 74
Plum-Cherry Saketini 75
Pyramid Point Pimm's Cup 70
Sake Cosmo 76
Scarlet Julep 97

·ST. PATRICK'S DAY
Eire-Cherr 103

·SUMMER DRINKS
Aurora Caipirinha 83
Bay Breeze 77
Beach Party 35
Cherry Bellini 58
Cherry Colada in Paradise 44
Cherry Mojito 36, 85
Flamingo 60
Lake Breeze 79
Lake Breeze-Virgin 37
Michigan Boston Cooler 44
Northern Lights Sangria 101
Power Island Iced Tea 70
Scarlet Sangria 102
Singapore Sling 71
Sparkling Cherry Lemonade 40
West End Beach 82

·SUSHI PARTY
Hari-Chari 78
Mandarin Cosmo 75
Pink Geisha Saketini 74
Plum-Cherry Saketini 75
Sake Cosmo 76
Samarai Sunrise 81

·TAILGATERS
Chocolate-Covered Cherry Ale 60
Mulled Cherry Wine 107
Mulled Cider 107
Red Eye 61
Red Wing 88
Traverse Cherry Bounce 65
Wassailing Cherries 88

TEA PARTIES
Ballet Slippers 34
Shirley Temple 40

·THANKSGIVING
Candy Apple 94
Cran-Cherry Tea Hot Punch 53
Mulled Cherry Wine 107
Mulled Cider 107
Ruby Slippers 101
Wassailing Cherries 88

·UPTOWN
Algonquin Tart 93
Aurora Caipirinha 83
Betty Paige 66
Cherry Mojito 85
Joyce's Very Cherry Cosmo 74
Lady Brett 103
Mandarin Cosmo 75
Pink Geisha Saketini 74
Pink Mink Martini 75
Pink Pussycat 69
Plum-Cherry Saketini 75
Sake Cosmo 76
Scarlet Gimlet 81
The Red Carpet 61

·VALENTINE'S
Ballet Slippers 34
Cherry-Chocolate Martini 74
Cherry-Vanilla TraVini 73
Cherry Fizzle Punch 99
Chocolate-Cherry Kiss 78
Pink Mink Martini 75
Pink Pussycat 69
Ruby Slippers 101

·WINTER DRINKS
Brandy Hot Chocolate 104
Hot Buttered Rum 105
Hot Cherry-Chocolate 53
Hot Toddy 106
Shanny's Brandy Alexander 71
Warm Ginger 54, 109

CHERRY DRINK TIPS

Use only 100 percent cherry juice or concentrate. Check product labels to ensure they don't contain other fruit juices or artificial flavorings.

•

Montmorency cherry juice and concentrates is recommended.

•

Mix 1 oz. concentrate in 7 oz. water to make juice.

•

Experiment with these drinks—adjust cherry to taste.

•

Cherry juice and concentrate can be substituted for one another in many drinks. Adjust amounts to taste.

•

Many recipes (particularly punches) can be adapted to include or exclude alcohol.

•

Cherry can be substituted in most drinks that call for grenadine or cranberry juice. It mixes well in drinks using lime, orange, pineapple, colas, chocolate, lemon-lime soda and vanilla liqueurs.

•

When mixed with dairy products, concentrate can change drink consistency. Mix well and consume relatively quickly.

•

In recipes that call for muddling, gently mash ingredients together using a muddler, pestle or spoon in the bottom of a glass or pitcher.

BAR MEASUREMENTS

1 dash/splash	=	1/32 ounce
1 teaspoon (tsp.)	=	1/8 ounce
1 tablespoon (Tbs.)	=	3/8 ounce
1 shot*	=	1½ ounces
1 fifth	=	26 ounces (1/5 gallon)

*A shot glass or jigger is usually 1.5 ounces, but sometimes 2 ounces with a measuring line at 1.5 ounces. Short shots or pony shots—used in martinis, Manhattans and Rob Roys—are 1 ounce.

PART I
SOFT DRINKS

JUICES & SPARKLERS

AT THE BEACH
Makes one drink

1 oz. cherry concentrate
3 oz. orange juice
3 oz. pineapple juice

Stir together over ice. Garnish with an orange slice
and cherry.

APPLE-CHERRY
Makes one drink

1 oz. cherry concentrate
10 oz. apple juice

Add concentrate to juice. Mix well.

—Amon Orchards

BALLET SLIPPERS
Makes one drink

1 glass sparkling white grape juice
2 tsp. cherry concentrate
1 Tbs. sugar

Pour 1 tsp. cherry concentrate onto saucer. Pour sugar onto separate saucer. Lightly dip champagne glass rim in cherry concentrate, then into sugar. Gently pour remaining cherry concentrate into bottom of glass. Slowly add sparkling grape juice.

•This is an alcohol-free version of Pink Slippers (a classic Kir Royale, or champagne cocktail). It's an unrivaled princess drink—enchanting, sparkle-rimmed, bubbly—and also fit for grown-up celebrations, whether they call for tiaras or not.

—Raymell English

BAY BREEZE, VIRGIN
Makes one drink

5 oz. pineapple juice
Splash cranberry juice
1 tsp. cherry concentrate
1 lime
1 cherry

Mix juices and cherry concentrate together in rocks glass. Add ice. Garnish with lime and cherry.

•Variation: Add a dose of sparkling water or club soda to create a spritzer.

34

BEACH PARTY
Makes one drink

1 Tbs. cherry concentrate
2 oz. orange juice
2 oz. pineapple juice
2 oz. lemon-lime soda
1 cherry
1 orange slice

Mix in tall glass. Add ice. Garnish with cherry, orange.

CHERRYADE
Makes two drinks

3 oz. cherry juice
    (Cairn Side recommended)
3 oz. lemonade

Mix together, add ice and serve.

—Donna Paradis, Cairn Side Juice

CHERRY CIDER
Makes one drink

2 Tbs. cherry concentrate
8 oz. apple cider

Stir together in tall glass over ice.

—Herb Teichman, Tree-Mendus Fruit

CHERRY FIZZ
Makes one 8-ounce drink

1 Tbs. cherry concentrate
1 tsp. honey
6 oz. club soda or sparkling water
1 fresh Bing cherry

In an 8-ounce glass, mix cherry concentrate and honey together. Pour in club soda and add ice. Garnish with fresh Bing cherry.

—Richard Beichner, executive chef,
Grand Traverse Resort & Spa

35

CHERRY MOJITO (LIBRE)
Makes one drink

7-8 mint leaves
1 tsp. sugar
1 lime, sliced
1 Tbs. cherry concentrate
7 oz. club soda
Sprig of mint

Muddle mint, sugar and lime in tall glass. Fill with ice.
Add soda and cherry concentrate. Garnish with mint.

CHOCULA-CHERRY
Makes one drink

1 tsp. cherry concentrate
4 oz. chocolate milk

Stir together vigorously. •*Drink quickly—cherry can
congeal in milk. Variation: Substitute soy or rice milk.*
—Jackson Steele

CRANCHERRY
Makes one drink

1 oz. cherry concentrate
10 oz. cranberry juice

Add concentrate to juice. Mix well. *Variation: Substitute
sparkling water for half of cranberry juice to make spritzer.*
—Amon Orchards

EVIL PRINCESS
Makes one drink

1 oz. cherry juice
2 oz. grape juice
1 oz. apple juice
1 Tbs. vanilla syrup
1 Tbs. lemon juice
1 lime slice

Pour over ice, stir and garnish with a lime slice.

36

GRAPE-CHERRY
Makes one drink

1 oz. cherry concentrate
10 oz. grape juice

Add concentrate to juice. Mix well. *Variation: Substitute sparkling water for half of grape juice to make spritzer.*
—Amon Orchards

LAKE BREEZE, VIRGIN
Makes one drink

3 oz. orange juice
1½ oz. cranberry juice
1 tsp. cherry concentrate
1 lime
1 cherry

Mix juices and cherry concentrate together in rocks glass. Add ice. Garnish with lime and cherry, plus an umbrella. *Variation: Add 2 oz. club soda or sparkling water for effervescence.*

LEMON-CHERRY
Makes one drink

1 oz. cherry concentrate
10 oz. lemonade

Add concentrate to lemonade. Mix well. *Variation: Substitute sparkling water for half of lemonade to make spritzer.*
—Amon Orchards

ORANGE-CHERRY
Makes one drink

1 oz. cherry concentrate
10 oz. orange juice

Add concentrate to juice. Mix well. *Variation: Substitute sparkling water for half of orange juice to make a spritzer.*
—Amon Orchards

PRETTY IN PINK
Makes one drink

1 tsp. cherry concentrate
4 oz. milk

Stir together. *•Drink quickly—cherry can congeal in milk.*
Variation: Substitute soy or rice milk
—Zoe Milagro Hall

RADIO FLYER
Makes one drink

4 oz. cream soda
1 tsp. cherry concentrate

Stir together over ice. *•Best in summer, with a straw.*
Double ingredients for grown-ups.
—Jackson Steele

REAL CHERRY 7-UP
Makes one drink

8 oz. 7-Up
1 oz. cherry concentrate

Stir together in tall glass over ice.

•Several people contributed this classic old-school
recipe. Mary Teichman recommended it for summer, saying,
"Cherry just gives 7-Up a nice spark, and it's very thirst-
quenching." Mary A. Smith noted that it's "always a real
refreshing but not sickening sweet kind of drink."
—Mary Teichman and
Mary A. Smith

REAL CHERRY COKE
Makes one 12-ounce soda

2 Tbs. cherry concentrate
12 oz. cola

Stir together in tall glass over ice.
—Richard Stearns, Sunrise Dried Fruit

38

RED LIGHT STOP!
Makes one 4-ounce drink

1 oz. cherry juice
3 oz. orange soda

Mix together. •*Best served with straw. Double portions for grown-ups.*

—Jackson Steele

RUBY SPRITZER
Makes one 6-ounce drink

3 oz. cherry juice
(Cairn Side recommended)
3 oz. 7-Up

Stir together in tall glass over ice.

—Bill Briggs, Cairn Side Juice

RUSSIAN CHERRY-LEMON
Makes three cups

1 cup cherry juice
2 Tbs. lemon juice
3 Tbs. sugar
2 cups milk
Dash salt

In enamel pan on stove, combine cherry juice and lemon juice. Add sugar. Stir until dissolved. Add salt to taste. Stir in. Bring mixture to a boil on low heat for 5 minutes. Remove from heat and cool. Add cold milk. Mix vigorously in mixer. Serve cold.

RUSTY SUPER-POWERED GINGER BLASTER
Makes one drink

4 oz. ginger ale
1 tsp. cherry concentrate

Mix together over ice. •*Best in summertime with a straw..*

—Jackson Steele

SHIRLEY TEMPLE
Makes one drink

¾ cup lemon-lime soda
1 Tbs. cherry concentrate
1 dash grenadine
1 stemmed maraschino cherry

In a tall glass, pour soda over ice. Add cherry concentrate and grenadine syrup. Stir well. Top with a maraschino cherry. Serve with straw.

•*Judy served this at her first Ravishing Red Hatters tea and it was a hit. "It's pretty and refreshing — great for a garden tea party," she says.*
—Judy Friske Kehr, Friske's Farm Market

SODA SHOP COLA
Makes one drink

¼ tsp. vanilla extract
½ tsp. cherry concentrate
6 oz. cola
Lemon wedge

Mix together, add ice and garnish with lemon.
—Jackson Steele

SPARKLING CHERRY LEMONADE
Makes 6-8 servings

2 Tbs. cherry concentrate
2 cups water
1 cup sugar
4 cups sparkling water
2 Tbs. grenadine
1 cup lemon juice
24 frozen tart cherries

In pitchers, mix cherry concentrate, water, sugar, sparkling water, grenadine and lemon juice well. Serve in individual glasses over ice. Float 3 frozen red tart cherries in each glass.

40

•This recipe was inspired by the first Very Cherry Drink Contest held during the National Cherry Festival in 2003. Although it wasn't the winner, Judy says it became a hit all summer at Friske's Orchard Cafe.

—Judy Friske Kehr, Friske's Farm Market

41

BLENDED DRINKS

BERRY CHERRY

Makes two drinks

½ cup fresh Montmorency (or other sour) cherries
½ cup cherry juice
1/3 cup frozen blueberries
1/3 cup sparkling apple juice
½ cup crushed ice

Combine all ingredients in blender; blend until smooth.

—Nancy McIntosh, McIntosh Orchard

42

CHERRY FRAPPUCINO
Makes three 7-ounce drinks

1 cup ice
2 scoops cherry ice cream
1 scoop coffee ice cream
1 Tbs. chocolate syrup
1 shot espresso or ¼ cup strong coffee
1/3 cup whole or skim milk

Spin it all together and drink away. *•Variation: Top with whipped cream, drizzle with chocolate syrup and garnish with a fresh tart cherry. This icy rich drink won kudos in the 2003 Very Cherry Drink Contest held at the National Cherry Festival in Traverse City. Cherry Republic, its creator, is known as a pioneering cherry cheerleader in northern Michigan, the nation's Cherry Capital.*

—Bob Sutherland, Cherry Republic

CHOCOLATE-CHERRY KISS
Makes one drink

2 oz. dark chocolate syrup
1 Tbs. cherry concentrate
2 scoops vanilla ice cream
Dash milk
Whipped cream
1 tart cherry

Slowly blend to milkshake consistency. Garnish with whipped cream, cherry. *•Drink quickly (but not so quickly that you get an ice cream headache).*

BLACK CHERRY MILKSHAKE
Makes one drink

1 oz. cherry concentrate
2 scoops vanilla ice cream
Dash milk

Slowly blend to milkshake consistency. *•Mix well and drink quickly.*

43

CHERRY COLADA IN PARADISE
Makes one drink

1 scoop ice
1 scoop vanilla malt ice cream
¾ oz. cherry concentrate
2 oz. pina colada mix
1 oz. pineapple juice
½ oz. heavy cream
Whipped cream
1 tart cherry

Blend. Garnish with whipped cream and cherry.
—North Peak Brewing Company

MICHIGAN BOSTON COOLER
Makes one drink

8 oz. Vernor's ginger ale
1 scoop vanilla ice cream
1 tsp. cherry concentrate

Blend well. Serve in tall glass with straw. •*Drink quickly.*
Historical note: The "Michigan" version of the Boston Cooler
allows only Michigan-made Vernor's, never other ginger ale.

SWEET & SOUR
Makes two drinks

1 cup cherry juice
¼ cup fresh Montmorency (or other
    sour) cherries, pitted
¼ cup fresh strawberries, sliced
½ cup crushed ice
½ tsp. lemon juice

Combine all ingredients in a blender until smooth.
Garnish with a frozen black cherry (pitted) or frozen
strawberry slices.
—Nancy McIntosh, McIntosh Orchard

44

CHERRY BOMB SMOOTHIE
Makes one 20-ounce drink

1 oz. cherry concentrate
5 strawberries
½ banana
2 Tbs. yogurt
1 tsp. honey
8 oz. freshly squeezed orange juice
1 cup ice

Place all ingredients in blender and blend until smooth. Serve in tall glass. •*Says Chris: "This is a great local drink—and good for you, too."*
—Chris Edson, Edson Farms Natural Foods

COLADA SMOOTHIE
Makes three 7-ounce drinks

1 banana
1½ cups frozen tart cherries
6 oz. limeade
¼ cup ice
¼ cup pina colada mix
2 Tbs. grated coconut

Place all ingredients in blender and blend until smooth.
—Bob Sutherland, Cherry Republic

FRUITY SMOOTHIE
Makes one drink

1 oz. cherry concentrate
8 oz. water
1 banana, peeled and sliced
¾ cups frozen peaches
(or other fruit)
½ cup frozen raspberries
(or other fruit)

Place all ingredients in blender, add ice and blend.
—Leelanau Fruit Company

45

ICE CREAM SMOOTHIE
Makes two 8-ounce servings

1 cup frozen tart cherries
½ cup cherry juice
1 cup vanilla ice cream

Puree cherries and juice until almost smooth. Add ice cream one third at a time; blend well. •*Drink quickly.*
—Cherry Marketing Institute

ORGANIC SOY SMOOTHIE
Makes four servings

3 cups organic soy milk
    (Eden recommended)
2 cups ice cubes
1/3 cup organic cherry concentrate
    (Eden recommended)

Place ingredients in a blender and pulse until ice is crushed. *Variation: Add a dash of organic maple syrup for a sweeter taste.*
—Eden Foods

SOY SMOOTHIE
Makes one 12-ounce drink

8 oz. chilled light organic vanilla-flavored
    soy milk
1 banana
6 oz. cherry yogurt
1 cup frozen sweet cherries
1 Tbs. frozen orange juice (undiluted)

Puree all ingredients in blender until smooth. Top with cherry.

    •*Sandra began making this after moving to the gorgeous coastal town of Northport, Michigan, located at the tip of the Leelanau Peninsula. She says: "It's great in summer and my granddaughters really like it."*
—Sandra Biagini

46

SIMPLE SMOOTHIE
Makes two 8-ounce servings

2 cups frozen tart cherries
1 ripe banana, peeled
1 cup cherry juice

Puree all ingredients until smooth.

—Cherry Marketing Institute

SUPERPOWER SMOOTHIE
Makes two servings

6 oz. orange juice
1 banana
1 oz. cherry juice concentrate
½ oz. wild blueberry concentrate
½ oz. pomegranate concentrate
2 oz. sliced strawberries
2 Tbs. protein powder
1 Tbs. flax seed powder

Blend ingredients with 4 ice cubes until smooth.
•Brownwood Acres cherry, blueberry and pomegranate concentrates recommended.

—Steve deTar, Brownwood Acres

TOFU SMOOTHIE
Makes three 8-ounce servings

2 cups frozen tart cherries, thawed
    and drained
1 (12.3-oz.) pkg. light silken tofu, cut up
¾ cup cherry juice
2 Tbs. honey
9 frozen or canned tart cherries

In a blender, combine cherries, tofu, cherry juice and honey. Cover; blend until smooth. Pour into 3 glasses. If desired, thread 3 cherries on each of three 6-inch bamboo skewers to garnish beverages. Serve immediately.

—Cherry Marketing Institute

47

YOGURT SMOOTHIE NO. 1
Makes one serving

8 oz. vanilla yogurt
1 oz. cherry concentrate
1 banana
½ cup frozen raspberries (or other fruit)
¼ cup frozen peaches (or other fruit)

Place in blender. Add ice to fill. Blend.

—Amon Orchards

YOGURT SMOOTHIE NO. 2
Makes two 8-ounce servings

1 cup plain or vanilla yogurt
1 ripe banana, peeled and sliced
½ cup orange juice
¼ cup cherry concentrate
1 cup crushed ice

Puree ingredients until smooth. Serve immediately.
•*This treat can be frozen in popsicle containers.*

—Cherry Marketing Institute

CHERRY ROYAL
Makes one drink

1 oz. cherry concentrate
1 can chocolate Slim Fast

Blend with ice.

—Leelanau Fruit Company

CHERRY SLIMFAST SHAKE
Makes one serving

1 scoop vanilla Slim Fast
1 oz. cherry juice concentrate
8 oz. skim milk
½ banana

Blend in blender until smooth.

—Leelanau Fruit Company

48

PUNCHES, TEAS & WARMER-UPPERS

CHERRY FIZZ PUNCH
Makes 6 servings

1 cup cherry juice
2 cups frozen tart cherries
1 six-oz. can frozen lemonade
6-8 ice cubes
1 twelve-oz. lemon-lime soda, chilled
Orange and lime slices

Puree cherry juice and frozen cherries until smooth.
Add lemonade concentrate and ice cubes; blend again
until smooth. Pour mixture into a 2-quart pitcher. Stir
in lemon-lime soda. Serve immediately; garnish with
orange and lime slices.

—Cherry Marketing Institute

49

CHERRY SANGRIA
Makes eight servings

2 cups white grape juice
2 cups orange juice
2 cups lemon-lime soda
2 cups cherry juice
4 orange slices
6 lime slices
8 cherries

Mix juices, soda together in glass pitcher. Float fruit on top. Serve in wine goblets for adults or kid-safe glasses.

•Variation: Substitute 1 oz. cherry concentrate plus 2 cups water or club soda for 2 cups cherry juice. Sparkling grape juice can also be used.

CHERRY SLUSH NO. 1
Makes 2 quarts

7 cups water
1 twelve-oz. can lemonade concentrate, thawed
1 twelve-oz. can orange juice concentrate, thawed
1 ½ cups sugar
1 cup cherry concentrate
1 two-liter bottle lemon-lime soda, chilled

In a large bowl, combine water, lemonade, orange juice and sugar. Stir until sugar is dissolved. Stir in cherry concentrate. Cover and freeze for at least 1-2 hours. Remove from freezer and thaw until mixture is slushy. To serve, mix equal amounts of slush and lemon-lime soda.

•Judy says: This is a great summer poolside drink or a festive holiday favorite.
—Judy Friske Kehr, Friske's Farm Market

CHERRY SLUSH NO. 2
Makes sixteen ¾-cup servings

2 cups cherry juice blend
1 cup granulated sugar
2 cups frozen tart cherries
1 six-oz. can frozen orange juice
concentrate, thawed
2 Tbs. lemon juice
1 two-liter lemon-lime soda, chilled

Combine cherry juice and sugar in medium saucepan. Cook over medium heat, stirring frequently, until mixture boils. Reduce heat; simmer 3 minutes. Remove from heat. In blender, combine cherries, orange juice concentrate and lemon juice. Blend 1 minute, or until cherries are pureed. In a 6-cup freezer container, combine cherry mixture and sugar mixture; mix well. Cover tightly; freeze 5 hours. Remove cherry mixture from freezer 30 minutes before serving. Put ¼ cup slush in each glass; add ½ cup soda to each. Serve immediately. Freeze remaining slush for later use.

—Cherry Marketing Institute

FESTIVE CHERRY PUNCH
Makes about 16 servings

1 can maraschino cherries
6-8 cups cherry juice, chilled
1 liter ginger ale, chilled

Make decorative ice ring ahead of time. Place ring or decorative mold in freezer; let chill. Rinse inside mold with cold water; return to freezer until thin ice coating forms. Cover bottom of mold in a decorative pattern with maraschino cherries. Gently add enough cherry juice to just cover fruit. Freeze until firm. Gently add more juice to fill mold completely. Freeze until firm. Just before serving, combine cherry juice blend and ginger ale in a large punch bowl. Add ice ring.

—Cherry Marketing Institute

51

ICED CHERRY-CITRUS GREEN TEA
Makes four servings

3 bags green tea (recommended are
    Eden's Organic Bancha Green Tea,
    Genmaicha (rice and green) Tea,
    Hojicha (roasted green) Tea, or
    Kukicha (roasted twig) Tea)
1 quart water
1/3 cup cherry concentrate (Eden
    Organic recommended)
4 orange slices
4 lemon slices
2 cups ice cubes

Place water in medium pot and bring to boil. Turn
off heat, add cherry concentrate, stir. Place tea bags in
water with strings hanging over pan's edge. Steep for 1
minute (over-steeping green tea produces bitter taste).
Place tea in pitcher; refrigerate until chilled. Pour into
glasses. Add ice, garnish with orange, lemon. *Variation: For sweeter flavor, add dash of organic maple syrup.*
                                                    —Eden Foods

ICED CHERRY SPARKLE TEA
Makes two quarts

4 cups sun tea or freshly brewed tea,
    slightly weak (do not over-steep)
3 cups cherry juice
1 cup fresh lemon juice
4 cups cold water
3 cups ginger ale

Chill tea in a 2- to 2½-quart glass pitcher. Just before
serving, stir in cherry juice, lemon juice, water (can
adjust to taste), and ginger ale. Add ice cubes to fill.

*•Freezing small pitted fresh cherries into ice cubes is
a colorful addition you can prepare ahead. For variations, try
different teas or use carbonated water in place of the ginger ale.*
                                    —Nancy McIntosh, McIntosh Orchard

52

CHERRY WASSAIL
Makes one drink

1 oz. cherry concentrate
10 oz. apple juice or cider
1 cinnamon stick

Stir ingredients together and heat.

—Leelanau Fruit Co.

CRAN-CHERRY TEA HOT PUNCH
Makes eight servings

8 bags tea, brewed in 4 cups water
2 cups cranberry juice
2 cups apple cider
¼ cup cherry concentrate
½ cup brown sugar
1 cinnamon stick
½ tsp. ginger
4 cloves

Brew tea on stove, add all ingredients, stir until sugar dissolves.

HOT CHERRY-CHOCOLATE
Makes one drink

8 oz. hot chocolate
1 tsp. cherry concentrate

Mix together. •*Prepackaged hot cocoa mixed with water is recommended as concentrate can congeal in milk.*

HOT CUP O' JOE
Makes one drink

6 oz. hot water
1 Tbs. cherry concentrate

Stir together. Adjust cherry concentrate to taste. •*Herb prefers this "cup o' joe" to morning coffee. You can add some mint, if you like, "to class it up a bit."*

—Herb Teichland, Tree-Mendus Fruit

53

HOT HONEY & CHERRY
Makes one drink

1 oz. cherry concentrate
1 Tbs. honey (or more, to taste)
10 oz. hot water

Mix together for a great warmer-upper.
— Leelanau Fruit Company

HOT SPICED CIDER
Makes one gallon

1 gallon apple cider
1 cup cherry concentrate
1 tsp. allspice
1 Tbs. cloves
2 cinnamon sticks

Combine all ingredients and let simmer for 1 hour or longer.

WARM GINGER
Makes one drink

8 oz. ginger ale (Vernor's recommended)
1 tsp. cherry concentrate

Stir together and warm on stove or in microwave.

PART II
HARD DRINKS

CHAMPAGNE, WINE & BEER

BLACK CHERRY SPRITZER
Makes one drink

5 oz. Piesporter
½ oz. cherry concentrate
Splash lemon-lime soda

In a tall cocktail glass, add ice, wine and cherry concentrate. Top with lemon-lime soda. Stir and garnish with black cherry and a lime wedge. *•Other white wines may be substituted. This drink's creators promise that it's ideal for a relaxing summer afternoon.*

—Mackinaw Brewing Company

CHERRY BELLINI
Makes one cocktail

3 oz. champagne
1 oz. cherry concentrate,
    mixed with 1 Tbs. simple syrup
¼ cup pitted tart cherries (frozen or
    fresh)
2 cups cracked ice
Whipped cream
Mint sprig

Reserve 1 cherry for garnish. Combine champagne, cherry concentrate, remaining cherries and ice in blender and puree to slushy consistency. Garnish with a dollop of whipped cream, a single tart cherry and mint sprig.

    •This exquisite drink is a derivative of the famous Bellini created by Giuseppe Cipriani at Harry's Bar in Venice in 1948, a cocktail inspired by 15th-century Venetian painter Giovanni Bellini. The original drink uses white peaches instead of cherries and is touted as an elegant sipper "for lazy times and beautiful people."

—Brad Klimaszewski, Amical

CHERRY FIZZ
Makes one cocktail

1 Tbs. cherry concentrate
1 tsp. honey
6 oz. demi-sec champagne or
    sparkling dry white wine
1 fresh Bing cherry

In an 8-oz. glass, stir together cherry concentrate and honey. Pour in champagne or wine. Garnish with fresh Bing, a sweet, black cherry. *•Bing cherries are America's favorite sweets. Variation: More cherry concentrate may be added for bolder flavor.*

—Richard Beichner, Grand Traverse Resort & Spa

58

Champagne, Wine & Beer

CHERRY KIR
Makes one cocktail

5 oz. white wine (Viognier
recommended)
1 tsp. cherry concentrate

Drizzle concentrate around interior of wine glass.
Gently add chilled wine.

*•This drink derives from the classic Kir, a white wine
flavored with a soupçon of cassis, or black currant, which is often served as an apéritif. See also Pink Slippers, an adaptation
of the Kir Royale, made with champagne, and Ballet Slippers, a
non-alcoholic version.*

—Tammi Elzinga

CRIMSON MIMOSA
Makes one cocktail

3 oz. champagne
2 oz. orange juice
1 oz. cherry juice
1 orange slice
1 cherry

Mix champagne, orange juice and cherry juice in
champagne glass. Garnish with orange slice and
cherry.

CHERRY-POM MIMOSA
Makes one cocktail

4 oz. dry champagne
½ oz. pomegranate juice
½ oz. cherry juice
½ oz. Cointreau
1 orange slice
1 cherry

Pour champagne into flute. Add pomegranate juice,
cherry juice and Cointreau. Garnish with orange slice,
cherry and umbrella.

59

CHOCOLATE-COVERED CHERRY ALE
Portions vary

Cherry mix:
    1 oz. cherry concentrate
    2 oz. water
Mission Point Porter

Stir cherry mix in desired quantities using 1-to-2 ratio.

PINT MIX: Stir together 1 oz. cherry mix and 15 oz. porter.

GROWLER BLEND: Stir together 4 oz. cherry mix and 60 oz. porter.

KEG BLEND: Stir 4 quarts of cherry mixture into keg.

—North Peak Brewing Company

FLAMINGO
Makes one cocktail

3 oz. chardonnay
3 oz. 7-Up or club soda
1 tsp. cherry concentrate
Lime wedge
2 cherries

Mix all ingredients together and garnish with pink umbrella, lime and cherries.

—Tammi Elzinga

PINK CHERRY BLOSSOM
Makes one drink

2 oz. cherry juice
    (Cairn Side recommended)
2 oz. champagne
    (Asti Santini recommended)

Combine in champagne flute.

—Sandra Paradis, Cairn Side Juice

Champagne, Wine & Beer

PINK SLIPPERS
(CHERRY KIR ROYALE)
Makes one drink

1 glass champagne
2 tsp. cherry concentrate
Sugar

Pour 1 tsp. cherry concentrate onto saucer. Pour sugar onto separate saucer. Dip champagne glass rim in cherry concentrate, then into sugar. Pour remaining cherry concentrate into bottom of glass. Slowly add champagne.

•This glamorous drink resembles the Kir Royale, champagne flavored with cassis, which is often served as an apéritif. See also Ballet Slippers, a non-alcoholic version.
—Raymell English

THE RED CARPET
(CLASSIC CHAMPAGNE COCKTAIL)
Makes one cocktail

2 dashes Angostura bitters
1 tsp. sugar
3 oz. champagne
1/3 oz. cognac
1 dash cherry concentrate
2 twists of lemon

Soak one sugar cube in a champagne flute with Angostura bitters. Add champagne, cognac and cherry concentrate. Squeeze in a twist of lemon and discard. Garnish with second twist of lemon

RED EYE
Makes one drink

1 bottle lager
1 tsp. cherry concentrate

Stir together in pint or pilsner glass.
—Ronald Hoge

SNAKEBITE RED
Makes one drink

4 oz. lager
4 oz. hard cider
1 Tbs. cherry concentrate

Stir together in pint glass.

•*This is a variation on a British pub classic, typically made with black currant juice. The combination of lager and cider, however, can be so lethal that some pubs ban the drink. This drink (and related variations, including Red Nasty and Red Witch) are favorites of the Goth crowd, though they're as well suited for a day on the boat as for Halloween.*

RED NASTY
Makes one drink

3 oz. lager
3 oz. hard cider
1 Tbs. cherry concentrate
½ oz. Pernod

Stir together in pint glass.

RED WITCH
Makes one drink

3 oz. lager
3 oz. hard cider
1 Tbs. cherry concentrate
1 oz. vodka

Stir together in pint glass.

RED RED WINE
Makes one drink

1 glass red wine (Shiraz recommended)
1 tsp. cherry concentrate

Drizzle cherry into wine glass. Pour in wine.

—Tammi Elzinga

LIQUEURS & CORDIALS

Homemade cherry liqueurs have a long history—from Russia to Hungary to northern Michigan—and there are as many recipe variations as there are orchards, it seems. Cherries are among the easiest fruits from which to create homemade flavored liquors—they often taste as good, or better, than commercially made liqueurs.

Antioxidants like melatonin are highly alcohol

soluble, so the health benefits remain even after cherries have soaked in vodka or brandy for a few months.

Bounces and cordials can be used in any recipe that calls for cherry liqueur.

CHERRY BOUNCE/CORDIAL
— WHISKEY—
Makes three quarts

2 quarts tart cherries
2 cups sugar
I fifth whiskey

Put together in glass container and let sit for four to six months.

•*Best served cold.*
—Becky Piazza, Miller's Family Orchard

TRAVERSE CHERRY BOUNCE
—VODKA—
Makes three quarts

I quart tart cherries
I½ cups sugar
I fifth vodka

Wash fresh cherries, leaving pits in. Break skins. Put in gallon jar. Add sugar and vodka. Stir until sugar dissolves. Let it sit (under bed) until Thanksgiving.

•*Best served cold.*
—Robert Hughes

CHERRY BOUNCE NO. 3
—RUM—
Makes three quarts

I quart tart cherries
I½ cups brown sugar
I fifth rum

Wash fresh cherries, leaving pits in. Break skins. Put in gallon jar. Add sugar and rum. Stir until sugar dissolves. Let it sit (under bed) until Thanksgiving.

•*Best served cold.*
—Robert Hughes

65

CHERRY BOUNCE NO. 4
— BRANDY—
Makes three quarts

1 quart tart cherries
1 ½ cups sugar
1 fifth brandy

Wash fresh cherries, leaving pits in. Break skins. Put in gallon jar. Add sugar and brandy. Stir until sugar dissolves. Let it sit (under bed) until Thanksgiving.

•*Best served cold.*

—Robert Hughes

CHERRY NALIVKA
Amounts vary

Fresh tart cherries
Vodka
Sugar

This Russian classic is similar to cherry liqueurs. Fill a large glass jug or bottle to the top with fresh cherries that have been washed and dried—in the sun—for two days. Fill the jug with vodka. Let sit for 1-2 months in dark place, then filter into smaller bottles and cork them. When drinking, add sugar to taste.

•*Variations: Other berries can be mixed with cherries, including apricots, apples, pears, blueberries, black currant, strawberries, etc.*

BETTY PAIGE
Makes one cocktail

1 oz. dry vermouth
1 oz. gin
1 tsp. cherry liqueur (or concentrate)
1 cherry

Shake vermouth and gin together. Pour into cocktail glass and add cherry liqueur. Garnish with cherry.

BLACK CHERRY
Makes one cocktail

2 oz. cherry juice (Cairn Side
  recommended)
1 oz. blackberry brandy
1 oz. lemonade

Combine ingredients and serve over ice in rocks glass.
—Mat and Leah Nicholson, Cairn Side Juice

CAFE KIRSCH
Makes one cocktail

1 oz. Kirschwasser or cherry liqueur
2 oz. cold black coffee
1 oz. sugar syrup
½ oz. egg white

Shake well and strain into a cocktail glass.

CAIRN SIDE SUNRISE
Makes one cocktail

2 oz. cherry juice (Cairn Side
  recommended)
2 oz. orange juice
2 oz. peach schnapps

Combine ingredients and serve over ice in rocks glass.
—Mat and Leah Nicholson, Cairn Side Juice

CAPTAIN'S TABLE
Makes one cocktail

½ oz. Campari
2 oz. gin
1 tsp. cherry concentrate
1 oz. orange juice
4 oz. ginger ale
1 cherry

Shake Campari, gin, cherry concentrate, orange juice
with ice. Strain into a tall glass nearly filled with ice.
Top with ginger ale. Garnish with cherry.

CHERRY COBBLER
Makes one cocktail

1 Tbs. sugar
2 oz. sparkling water
1 Tbs. cherry concentrate
2 oz. sherry
1 cherry

Dissolve sugar, cherry concentrate in sparkling water.
Add cracked ice. Add sherry. Garnish with cherry.

CHERRY CREAMSICLE
Makes one drink

2 oz. vanilla liqueur
4 oz. cherry juice
2 oz. half & half
1 cherry

Shake together with ice. Strain into a chilled rocks
glass. Garnish with cherry. Drink quickly.

—Ronald Hoge

CHERRY SIDECAR
Makes one cocktail

1½ shots cognac or brandy
½ shot Cointreau or Triple Sec
1 lemon, squeezed
1 tsp. cherry concentrate

Shake with ice; strain into glass. Sugared rim optional.

CLASSIC FIZZ
Makes one cocktail

2 oz. cherry brandy
½ lemon, squeezed
2 oz. sparkling water
1 cherry

Shake lemon juice, ice, brandy. Strain over ice cubes.
Stir in sparkling water. Garnish with cherry.

HUMMER
Makes one cocktail

½ oz. bourbon
½ oz. cherry liqueur
1 oz. heavy cream
1 oz. light rum

Shake well with ice. Strain into a cocktail or rocks glass.

NALGAA
Makes one cocktail

2 shots Campari
2 Tbs. cherry liqueur
2 shots lemon-lime soda

In rocks glass, place 4 ice cubes. Pour in cherry liqueur. Add Campari. Add soda.

NUTS & CHERRIES
Makes one cocktail

1 shot cherry brandy
1 shot Frangelico
1 shot heavy cream

Layer ingredients over ice in rocks glass.

•This is a variation on one of Susan's favorite late-night college-era treats, Nuts & Berries, which features chambord in place of cherry brandy. "The drink has a smooth Kahlua and cream feel to it," she says.
—Susan Littlefield-Dungjen

PINK PUSSYCAT
Makes one cocktail

2 oz. Alize Red Passion
2 oz. pineapple juice
½ tsp. cherry concentrate

Mix together in rocks glass. Add ice.

69

POWER ISLAND ICED TEA
Makes one drink

½ oz. vodka
½ oz. rum
½ oz. gin
½ oz. tequila
½ oz. Triple Sec
½ oz. cherry concentrate
Splash of lemon-lime soda
Splash of sweet & sour mix
1 cherry
1 lime wedge

In a tall cocktail glass, build on ice, spirits and cherry concentrate. Stir and top with lemon-lime soda; finish with a splash of sweet & sour. Garnish with a cherry and wedge of lime.

•*Power Island, rising in the midst of West Grand Traverse Bay and accessible only by boat, is the party destination for those who desire full-tilt summer pleasure. Mackinaw Brewing says its Power Island Iced Tea "supplies a full measure of party attitude with a very cherry kick."*
—Mackinaw Brewing Company

PYRAMID POINT PIMM'S CUP
Makes one cocktail

2 oz. Pimm's No. 1
1 tsp. cherry concentrate
1 slice cucumber
3 oz. ginger ale
1 slice lemon

Pour Pimm's into pint glass, fill with ice, stir in cherry concentrate. Top with chilled ginger ale. Garnish with slice of lemon and a slice of cucumber.

•*This peculiar spring quaff with its brash cucumber garnish was a 19th-century invention favored by Brits at cricket matches.*

PURPLE MOTORCYCLE
Makes one cocktail

1½ oz. tequila
1½ oz. rum
1½ oz. vodka
1½ oz. gin
1½ oz. blue curaçao
1 Tbs. cherry concentrate
1 splash 7-Up
1 oz. sweet and sour mix
1 cherry

Over ice in tall glass, add liquors, cherry concentrate. Stir. Fill with sour mix; add 7-Up. Garnish with cherry.

SHANNY'S BRANDY ALEXANDER
Makes one cocktail

1½ oz. cherry brandy
1½ oz. crème de cacao
1½ oz. heavy cream

Shake ingredients with ice, strain into brandy or rocks glass. *Variation: Top with whipped cream, swirl with chocolate.*
—Shannon Hall

SINGAPORE SLING
Makes one cocktail

1½ oz. gin
½ oz. cherry brandy
¼ oz. Cointreau
¼ oz. Benedictine
4 oz. pineapple juice
½ oz. lime juice
½ oz. grenadine
Dash bitters
1 cherry

Shake with ice. Strain into a tall ice-filled glass. Garnish with cherry. *Variation: Substitute 1 Tbs. cherry concentrate for grenadine.*

71

SWEET DREAMS
Makes one cocktail

3 oz. cherry juice (Cairn Side
   recommended)
1½ oz. Amaretto
1½ oz. peach schnapps

Combine ingredients and serve over ice in rocks glass.
—Mat and Leah Nicholson, Cairn Side Juice

VERY PINK SQUIRREL
Makes one cocktail

1 oz. crème de cacao
1 oz. crème de noyaux
½ oz. cherry liqueur
1 oz. heavy cream

Shake with crushed ice. Strain into a chilled cocktail
glass.

YOUR CHERRY, MY CHERRY
Makes one cocktail

Chocolate syrup
½ oz. Bailey's Irish cream
½ oz. Godiva chocolate liqueur
½ oz. Amaretto
½ oz. cherry brandy

Swirl chocolate syrup or ganache into cocktail glass.
Shake Irish cream, chocolate liqueur, Amaretto and
cherry brandy together with ice and strain into glass.
—Bruce Liable, Big Eazy

VODKA

CHERRY-VANILLA TRAVINI
Makes one cocktail

½ oz. vanilla vodka (Absolut
recommended)
½ oz. Cheri-Beri Pucker
1 oz. tart cherry juice

Combine in a hand shaker over ice. Shake and strain
into a large martini glass.

•*Drink creator Michael Trubac says, "We have many
hand-shaken TraVinis (martinis) on our menu and the Cherry
Vanilla TraVini is one of the most popular. This recipe was
the winner of the gold award for the Very Cherry Drink Contest Alcohol Category of the 2003 National Cherry Festival."*
—Michael Trubac, TraVino Traverse Wine and Grille

73

CHERRY-CHOCOLATE MARTINI
Makes one drink

1 oz. vodka (Kettle One recommended)
1 oz. white crème de cacao
1 oz. dark crème de cacao
¼ oz. cherry concentrate (Michelle's
    Miracle Cherry Concentrate
    recommended)

Shake together with ice. Strain into martini glass.
—Michelle White, Leland Cherry Company
Inspired by martini at Riverside Inn in Leland, Michigan

JOYCE'S VERY CHERRY COSMOPOLITAN
Makes one cocktail

1½ oz. vodka
    (Kettle One recommended)
¼ oz. Cointreau
¾ oz. lime juice
    (Rose's recommended)
1 cup cherry juice (made with 1 oz.
    Michelle's Miracle Cherry
    Concentrate)
1 orange slice

Shake all ingredients together with ice. Serve in martini glass garnished with an orange slice.
—Joyce Lalonde

PINK GEISHA SAKETINI
Makes one cocktail

½ oz. sake
1½ oz. vanilla vodka
½ oz. crème de cacao
1 dollop cherry concentrate
2 fresh cherries

Shake sake, vodka, crème de cacao and cherry concentrate together with ice in cocktail shaker. Strain into cocktail glass. Garnish with cherries, pink umbrella.

74

PINK MINK MARTINI
Makes one cocktail

1 lime wedge
2 shots cherry juice (100 percent pure,
    of course)
1 heavy shot vodka (Grey Goose
    recommended)
½ shot Cointreau
½ shot Grand Marnier

Squeeze lime into shaker. Add ice and remaining ingredients. Shake like mad. Strain off into large pre-chilled cocktail glass.

•Variations: Earlier incarnations of this drink contained a dash of Angostura bitters. This delicate drink with lots of bling was served by the Sutherlands at a cocktail party celebrating a local production of "The Vagina Monologues."
—Matt and Victoria Sutherland

MANDARIN COSMO
Makes one cocktail

1½ oz. Absolut Mandarin Vodka
½ oz. Cointreau
1 splash lime juice
1 splash cherry juice

Shake together with chipped ice, strain into chilled cocktail glass.

PLUM-CHERRY SAKETINI
Makes one cocktail

½ oz. plum sake
2½ oz. vodka
½ oz. cherry juice
Lemon twist

Shake together with ice. Strain into chilled cocktail glass. Garnish with lemon twist.

75

SAKE COSMO
Makes one cocktail

Lemon wedge
1 Tbs. sugar
2½ oz. Tentaka Kuni sake
½ oz. Cointreau
¼ lime, squeezed
¼ oz. cherry juice
Lime twist

Run lemon around edge of a chilled cocktail glass.
Dip rim into sugar. Shake sake, Cointreau, lime, cherry
juice with ice. Strain into glass. Garnish with lime.

•*This springtime cocktail was created for the 2004
Cherry Blossom Festival in Washington, D.C. Saketinis, made
with rice wine, are less harsh tasting than traditional martinis.*
—Austin Pham and Derek Brosseau,
Garden Terrace Lounge, Four Seasons Hotel

SOUR CHERRY MARTINI
Makes one cocktail

1 shot of Stoli strawberry vodka
¾ shot Cherry Pucker
1 shot cherry juice

Shake until crystals form; strain into chilled martini
glass. Garnish with cherry.
—Teresa Sullivan

WILD CHERRY LIFESAVER MARTINI
Makes one mixed drink

3 oz. Grey Goose vodka
1 Tbs. cherry concentrate

Pour chilled vodka into martini glass. Add a generous
splash of cherry concentrate.

•*Says Melanie: "So yummy, it is dangerous."*
—Melanie Drane

76

AFTERNOON DELIGHT
Makes one cocktail

1 shot vodka
1 oz. cherry juice
20 ice cubes
2 shots Fresca

In, blender, mix vodka, cherry juice and ice into a slush. Add Fresca, blend again.

—Mary Waller, Brownwood Acres

ATOMIC CHERRY
Makes one cocktail

1 shot vodka
1 Tbs. cherry concentrate
1½ oz. orange juice
1½ oz. club soda

Mix ingredients, add ice, garnish with lime.

—Raymell English

BAY BREEZE
Makes one cocktail

2 oz. vodka
5 oz. pineapple juice
Splash cranberry juice
1 tsp. cherry concentrate

Mix vodka, juices and cherry concentrate together in rocks glass. Add ice. *Optional garnishes: Lime, cherry.*

CHERRY BOMB
Makes one cocktail

2 shots cherry juice
(Cairn Side recommended)
1 shot vodka

Combine in cocktail glass with ice. Garnish with cinnamon stick.

—Tom and Karen Paradis, Cairn Side Juice

77

CHERRY SCREWDRIVER
Makes one cocktail

1 shot vodka
3 oz. orange juice
1 Tbs. cherry concentrate

Stir together; add ice.

CHOCOLATE-CHERRY KISS
Makes one drink

1 shot vodka
1 shot crème de cacao
2 scoops vanilla ice cream
1 tsp. cherry concentrate

Blend together vodka, crème de cacao, ice cream and cherry concentrate until smooth. Pour into parfait or rocks glass. *Variation: Top with whipped cream, drizzle with chocolate syrup, and garnish with a cherry on top. Drink quickly.*

—Terry VanKleek

FIRE ENGINE
Makes one cocktail

1 shot vodka
2 shots 7-Up
1 Tbs. cherry concentrate

Serve mixed together on the rocks.

—Billy Hoxie

HARI-CHARI (CHERRY KAMIKAZE)
Makes one cocktail

1 oz. lime juice
1 oz. Triple Sec
1 oz. vodka
1 tsp. cherry concentrate

Shake and serve over ice in rocks glass.

I LOVE LUCY
Makes one cocktail

1 oz. vodka
2 oz. club soda
1 tsp. grenadine
1 Tbs. cherry concentrate

Mix together over ice. *Variation: Add juice of 1 lime slice.*

JOHNNIE'S CHERRY BOMB
Makes one cocktail

1 oz. vodka
½ oz. cherry concentrate (Michelle's
    Miracle recommended)
6 oz. water or soda
Lemon or lime slice

Mix together over ice, add lemon or lime garnish
　　　　　—John Vidergar, Leland Cherry Company

LAKE BREEZE
Makes one cocktail

2 oz. vodka
3 oz. orange juice
1½ oz. cranberry juice
1 tsp. cherry concentrate

Mix in rocks glass. Add ice. *Variation: Garnish with lime and cherry.*

LAVA LAMP
Makes one cocktail

1 shot vodka
2 shots club soda
1 lime slice
1 Tbs. cherry concentrate

Squeeze lime into rocks glass. Stir in vodka, club soda.
Add 4 ice cubes. Slowly drizzle concentrate into drink.
　　　　　—Ronald Hoge

79

PITTY
Makes one cocktail

2 oz. vodka
1 oz. Kirschwasser
1 oz. orange juice
1 tsp. cherry concentrate

Mix together. Add ice. *Optional: Garnish with cherry.*
—Ronald Hoge

PITILESS
Makes one cocktail

2 oz. 200-proof vodka
1 oz. Kirschwasser
1 oz. orange juice
1 tsp. cherry concentrate

Mix together. Add ice. *Optional: Garnish with cherry.*
—Ronald Hoge

RED FISH, BLUE FISH
Makes one cocktail

1 shot club soda
1 shot vodka
1 shot blue curaçao
1 Tbs. cherry concentrate

Stir vodka, club soda, curaçao together. Add ice. Gently dribble in cherry concentrate.

RED, WHITE & BLUE
Makes one cocktail

1 Tbs. cherry concentrate
1 shot vodka
1 shot 7-Up
½ shot blue curaçao

Pour cherry concentrate into rocks glass. Add ice. Gently add vodka, 7-Up. Gently add curaçao.
—Raymell English

SAMURAI SUNRISE
Makes one cocktail

1 shot vodka
1 shot light rum
1 Tbs. cherry concentrate
3 oz. orange juice

Pour vodka and rum over ice in a tall glass. Tilt the glass; slowly pour cherry concentrate down the interior. Gently fill with chilled orange juice.

SCARLET GIMLET
Makes one cocktail

1½ oz. vodka
1½ oz. lime juice, freshly squeezed
1 Tbs. cherry concentrate

Mix together in highball glass, on the rocks.

—Sherwood Smith

SEX IN THE ORCHARD
(CHERRY SEX ON THE BEACH)
Makes one cocktail

1 oz. vodka
1 oz. peach schnapps
2 oz. orange juice
2 oz. cranberry juice
1 tsp. cherry concentrate

Stir together in tall glass with ice.

SNAPDRAGON
Makes one cocktail

¼ oz. cherry concentrate
Splash of Sprite
1½ oz. Stoli Vanilla vodka

Shake with ice and strain into martini glass.

—Leigh McKolay and Nabiel Musleh
Minerva's / Beacon Lounge

81

SOUR CHERRY
Makes one drink

1 lemon, juiced
2 oz. vodka
½ tsp. powdered sugar
1 tsp. cherry concentrate
1 orange slice
1 cherry

Shake ingredients with ice and strain into glass. Garnish with half-slice of orange and cherry. *Variations: Substitute sour mix for lemon, powdered sugar.*

WEST END BEACH
Makes one cocktail

1 Tbs. cherry concentrate
1 oz. club soda
2 oz. orange juice
2 oz. pineapple juice
1 shot vodka

Fill tall glass with vodka, club soda, concentrate and juices. Garnish with cherry.

RUM

AURORA CAIPIRINHA
Makes one cocktail

1 lime
2 brown sugar cubes
2 oz. Cachaca rum
1 tsp. cherry concentrate

Cut the lime into eighths and place into a tall glass with the sugar cubes and muddle. Fill the glass with crushed ice and top with Cachaca. Stir and serve with a straw.

•This Brazilian specialty is a cousin of the popular Cuban mojito. Light rum can be substituted for Cachaca, a sugar cane rum.

83

CHERRY CUBA LIBRE

Makes one cocktail

2 oz. rum
3 oz. cola
1 Tbs. cherry concentrate
1 lime wedge

Mix over ice in a rocks glass. Squeeze in lime. Garnish with lime rind.

CHERRY CUBA LIBRE—SPICED

Makes one cocktail

2 oz. spiced rum
3 oz. vanilla cola
1 Tbs. cherry concentrate
1 lime wedge

Mix over ice in a rocks glass. Squeeze in lime.

CHERRY DAIQUIRI

Makes one cocktail

2 oz. golden rum
½ oz. fresh lime juice
½ oz. sugar syrup
1 Tsp. cherry concentrate

Shake with ice; strain into martini glass. *Frozen: Blend ingredients with ice.*

CHERRY MAI TAI — CLASSIC

Makes one cocktail

1 oz. light rum
1 oz. gold rum
½ oz. orange curaçao
1 Tbs. cherry concentrate
½ oz. fresh lime juice
1 oz. dark rum

Shake all but the dark rum with ice. Strain into rocks glass. Top with the dark rum. Garnish with a cherry.

CHERRY MAI TAI — FRUITY
Makes one cocktail

1 oz. light rum
½ oz. Triple Sec
¼ oz. lime juice
1½ oz. pineapple juice
1½ oz. orange juice
1 tsp. cherry concentrate
½ oz. dark rum

Shake all but the dark rum with ice. Strain into rocks glass. Top with the dark rum. Garnish with a cherry.

CHERRY MOJITO
Makes one cocktail

7-8 mint leaves
1 tsp. sugar
1 lime, sliced
2 oz. rum
1 tsp. Montmorency cherry concentrate
3 oz. club soda

Reserve 1 mint sprig for garnish. Muddle mint, sugar and lime in tall glass. Fill with crushed ice. Add rum, soda and cherry concentrate. Garnish with mint sprig. Serve with straws. •*This Cuban drink was popular in the 1910s and 1920s and recently became fashionable again.*

FRUIT SLUSH
Makes four servings

1 banana
¼ cup cherry concentrate
4 shots rum
½ cup strawberries
1 cup tart cherries
½ cup blueberries

Blend together. Add ice, blend again.
—Paulette Tilkington, Brownwood Acres

85

JIMMY BUFFET UP NORTH
Makes one cocktail

1 shot dark rum (Myer's recommended)
1 Tbs. cherry concentrate
Pineapple juice to fill

Mix together in highball glass with ice. Garnish with cherry.

LUCY & RICKY
Makes one cocktail

1 oz. dark rum
2 oz. club soda
1 Tbs. lime juice
1 Tbs. cherry concentrate

Stir together over ice into rocks glass.

MARY PICKFORD
Makes one cocktail

1 ½ oz. light rum
1 oz. pineapple juice
½ tsp. cherry liqueur
½ tsp. cherry concentrate

Shake well with ice, strain into a cocktail glass. Garnish with cherry.

MICHIGAN MULE
Makes one cocktail

1 shot spiced rum
Dash of fresh lime juice
Dash of sugar syrup
1 tsp. cherry concentrate
3 oz. ginger beer
1 lime wedge

Mix rum, lime juice, sugar syrup and cherry concentrate in a tall glass. Add ice. Top with ginger beer. Garnish with lime wedge.

NORTHERN SQUALL
(CHERRY HURRICANE)
Makes one cocktail

1½ oz. dark rum
1½ oz. light rum
2 oz. orange juice
2 oz. pineapple juice
1½ tsp. cherry concentrate
½ tsp. sugar
1 oz. 151-proof rum
2 cherries
1 pineapple chunk
1 sugar cube

Pour dark rum, light rum, orange juice, pineapple juice and cherry concentrate over ice into a large glass (pilsner or parfait are traditional). Add the half tsp. of sugar, stir slightly, and top with 151 rum. Garnish with cherries and pineapple. *Optional: Add sugar cube and light it up.*

•This is a very-cherry variation of New Orleans' classic cocktail, a staple on Bourbon Street and during Mardi Gras celebrations.

PINK WITCH
Makes one cocktail

2 oz. white rum
1 oz. white crème de cacao
1 oz. Cointreau
1 tsp. cherry concentrate
Splash soda water
1 orange slice
1 lime slice
1 cherry

Shake liquors, cherry concentrate and soda water together with ice, strain into tall glass. Garnish with orange, lime, cherry. Serve with straw.

RED WING
Makes one cocktail

2 oz. light rum
½ oz. Amaretto
½ oz. Triple Sec
1 oz. lime juice
½ Tbs. cherry concentrate

Combine all ingredients in cocktail shaker with cracked ice. Pour into chilled rocks glass. Garnish with cherry.

SPICED CHERRY MADRAS
Makes one cocktail

2 oz. spiced rum
1 oz. orange juice
1 oz. cranberry juice
1 tsp. cherry concentrate
1 lime wedge

Stir rum, juices and cherry concentrate together in rocks glass. Add ice. Garnish with lime wedge.

TART N' STORMY
Makes one cocktail

2 oz. Gosling's Black Seal rum
4 oz. ginger beer
1 Tbs. cherry concentrate

Mix in a rocks glass over cracked ice.

WASSAILING CHERRIES
Makes one drink

1 oz. cherry concentrate
10 oz. apple juice or cider
1 shot spiced rum
1 cinnamon stick

Stir cherry concentrate and apple juice or cider together and heat. Add cinnamon stick.

ZIPPY ZOMBIE
Makes one drink

1 tsp. brown sugar
1 oz. lemon juice
1 oz. lime juice
1 oz. pineapple juice
1 tsp. cherry concentrate
1 oz. passion fruit syrup
1 dash Angostura bitters
1 oz. golden rum
1 oz. 151-proof rum
1 oz. white rum
Mint sprig

In shaker, dissolve sugar in juices and concentrates. Add rums and bitters. Shake with ice and pour into a tall glass. Garnish with a mint sprig.

TEQUILA

CHERRYRITA
Makes one drink

1 oz. tequila (Hornitos recommended)
¾ oz. Grand Marnier
¾ oz. lime juice, freshly squeezed
1 oz. cherry concentrate
1 lime slice
1 tart cherry

Combine ingredients in a shaker cup filled with
cracked ice. Shake vigorously. Pour into a sugar-
rimmed glass with lime wheel and tart cherry garnish.
—Brad Klimaszewski, Amical

90

FIREBALL
Makes one cocktail

1 shot tequila
1 drizzle cherry juice
Tabasco to taste

Pour tequila into rocks glass. Drizzle in cherry juice.
Shake in Tabasco to taste.

—Terry VanKleek

MICHELLE'S CHERRY MARGARITA
Makes one drink

1 oz. tequila (Jose Cuervo)
1 oz. Cointreau
½ oz. Rose's lime juice
¼ oz. cherry concentrate (Michelle's
    Miracle recommended)
Salt
1 lime or orange slice

Shake or blend with ice. Salt the rim of glass, serve
with a lime or an orange garnish.

—Michelle White, Leland Cherry Company

PINK CADILLAC
Makes one cocktail

Salt
2 lime wedges
1 shot tequila gold
½ shot Cointreau
1 shot fresh lime juice
2 tsp. Grand Marnier
1 tsp. cherry concentrate

Salt rim of rocks or margarita glass: Squeeze one lime
wedge onto a saucer; shake salt onto a second saucer.
Dip glass rim first in lime juice, then in salt. Shake
remaining ingredients together with ice and strain into
glass. Garnish with remaining lime wedge.

91

NORTHERN FROSTBITE
Makes one cocktail

1 oz. tequila
¾ oz. white crème de cacao
¾ oz. heavy cream
1 Tbs. cherry concentrate

Shake ingredients hard with ice. Strain into a cocktail glass. Garnish with a sprinkle of nutmeg.

NORTHERN SUNRISE
Makes one cocktail

1 shot tequila
4 oz. orange juice
1 Tbs. cherry concentrate
1 lime wedge
1 cherry

Mix tequila, orange juice in rocks glass. Add ice cubes. Gently dribble cherry concentrate over top. Garnish with lime wedge, cherry.

WHISKEY

ALGONQUIN TART
Makes one cocktail

2 oz. Canadian whiskey
1 oz. dry vermouth
1 oz. pineapple juice
1 tsp. cherry concentrate
1 tart cherry
1 pineapple slice

Mix together whiskey, vermouth, pineapple juice, cherry concentrate over ice in rocks glass. Garnish with cherry and pineapple. •*A group of celebrated literary-world figures including Dorothy Parker met regularly at New York City's Algonquin Hotel from 1919-29.*

AQUARIAN CHERRY

Makes one cocktail

2 shots Scotch whiskey
1 shot cherry brandy liqueur
1½ shots of cranberry juice
¼ shot sugar syrup

Shake ingredients with ice and strain into ice-filled rocks glass.

CANADIAN CHERRY

Makes one cocktail

Bar sugar
1 oz. cherry brandy
2 oz. Canadian whiskey
2 tsp. lemon juice
2 tsp. orange juice

Pour dash of brandy into one saucer, sugar into another. Dip glass rim first into brandy, then sugar. Shake remaining ingredients with cracked ice and strain into glass.

CANDY APPLE

Makes one cocktail

1 oz. Old Crow bourbon
3 oz. apple cider
1 Tbs. cherry concentrate

Mix together with ice.

—Ronald Hoge

CHERRY SCOTTISH GUARD

Makes one cocktail

1½ oz. Scotch whiskey
½ oz. lemon juice
½ oz. orange juice
1 tsp. cherry concentrate

Shake with ice. Strain into a cocktail glass.

CHERRY WHISKEY SOUR
Makes one drink

1 lemon, juiced
2 oz. blended whiskey
½ tsp. powdered sugar
½ tsp. cherry concentrate
½ slice lemon
1 cherry

Shake ingredients with ice and strain into glass. Garnish with half-slice of lemon and cherry. •*Variation: Substitute sour mix for lemon, powdered sugar.*
—Ray "Mr. Cherry USA" Pleva

CRIMSON HIGHBALL
Makes one cocktail

1½ oz. whiskey
1 tsp. cherry concentrate
6 oz. ginger ale
1 cherry

Add ice to glass. Pour in whiskey. Stir in cherry concentrate. Add ginger ale. Garnish with cherry. •*In this classic drink, cherry enhances the flavor, adding "a little color, a little zip," says "Mr. Cherry USA." This northern Michigan interpretation of the highball is a favorite of one of his cousins.*
—Ray "Mr. Cherry USA" Pleva

DELMONICO, RARE
Makes one cocktail

1 oz. gin
½ oz. brandy
½ oz. dry vermouth
½ oz. sweet vermouth
1 tsp. cherry concentrate
1 dash orange bitters

Stir together with ice. Strain into a cocktail glass. Garnish with a lemon twist.

95

MISS AMERICAN PIE
Makes one cocktail

1 oz. whiskey
1 oz. rye
3 oz. cherry juice

Stir together over ice. Garnish with cherry.

—Timothy Hall

OLD MISSION MANHATTAN
Makes one cocktail

2 oz. rye or bourbon whiskey
½ oz. sweet vermouth
1 dash Angostura bitters
1 tsp. cherry concentrate

Stir together with ice. Strain into a cocktail glass.

•*Ray says: "This is for the 19th hole, when everyone's trying to tell you why they're the better golfer."*

—Ray "Mr. Cherry USA" Pleva

RED RHETT BUTLER
Makes one cocktail

1 oz. bourbon
2 oz. cranberry juice
1 tsp. sugar syrup
2 oz. cherry juice
¼ lime, squeezed

Shake ingredients with ice and strain into ice-filled rocks glass. Garnish with cherry on a cocktail stick.

RUBY ROB ROY
Makes one cocktail

1¾ oz. Scotch
½ oz. sweet vermouth
1 tsp. cherry concentrate
1 dash Angostura bitters

Mix ingredients. Garnish with cherry.

RUDDY SCOT (REALLY RUSTY NAIL)
Makes one cocktail

1 oz. Drambuie
1 oz. Scotch
1 Tbs. cherry concentrate

Fill rocks glass with ice. Add Drambuie, Scotch, cherry concentrate and stir.

VERY CHERRY OLD FASHIONED
Makes one cocktail

½ orange slice
1 cube or tsp., white sugar
2 dashes Angostura bitters
2 oz. rye or bourbon whiskey
1 tsp. cherry concentrate

Muddle orange, sugar, bitters together until the sugar is dissolved. Fill glass with ice, add whiskey, cherry concentrate. Stir. Garnish with a cherry, orange slice.

SCARLET JULEP
Makes one cocktail

3 fresh mint sprigs
1 tsp. sugar
¼ oz. water
1 tsp. cherry concentrate
1 oz. Kentucky bourbon

In a bowl, muddle 2 mint sprigs, sugar and water. Chill for 30 minutes. Fill chilled tumbler with crushed ice, stir together cherry concentrate and bourbon. Top with strained mint muddle. Garnish with mint sprig.

•*This genteel Southern drink is the classic cocktail for Derby days. Here, it gets a bold northern twist with cherry. Drink-making techniques for juleps are hotly debated by bartenders and regular folks alike—among chief disputes is whether to muddle or layer—but this recipe includes the basic ingredients that tend to be agreed upon by all.*

97

SUTTONS BAY OLD FASHIONED — SWEET

Makes one cocktail

1 tsp. sugar
2 dashes Angostura bitters
1 orange slice
1 pitted fresh or frozen sweet cherry
1½ shot bourbon

Muddle sugar, bitters, orange and cherry. Add bourbon, ice. Garnish with fresh cherry.

—Daniel H. Gorney, O'Keefe's Pub

SUTTONS BAY OLD FASHIONED — TART

Makes one cocktail

1 tsp. sugar
2 dashes Angostura bitters
1 orange slice
1 pitted fresh or frozen tart cherry
1½ shots Canadian whiskey

Muddle sugar, bitters, orange and cherry (using mortar and pestle, grind together in bottom of glass). Add whiskey, ice. Garnish with fresh cherry.

—Daniel H. Gorney, O'Keefe's Pub

TART WHISKEY SOUR

Makes one drink

2 oz. whiskey
½ lemon
½ tsp. powdered sugar
1 tsp. cherry concentrate
½ slice lemon
1 cherry

Shake whiskey, juice of lemon, powdered sugar and cherry concentrate with ice and strain into a glass. Garnish with half-slice of lemon and cherry.

PUNCH, SHOTS & HOT DRINKS

CHERRY FIZZLE PUNCH

Makes sixteen servings

2 liters 7-Up, Sprite, or Vernor's
Vodka to taste
16 oz. cherry concentrate

Mix ingredients together in a punch bowl.

•*Ray says, "That's a punch that's good all year round—Christmas, Valentine's, anniversaries, weddings. The red color really stands out."*

—Ray "Mr. Cherries USA" Pleva

99

FLAMING VOLCANO
Serves four

2 oz. dark rum
2 oz. golden rum
2 oz. light rum
2 oz. coconut rum
1 oz. cherry concentrate
3 oz. cranberry juice
4 oz. orange juice
4 oz. pineapple juice
8 cherries
6 orange slices
1 oz. 151-proof rum

Combine the first 4 rums with cherry concentrate and all of the juices in a super-size glass or a low bowl that you can drink from. Float cherries, oranges in bowl. Place 151-proof rum in a separate small glass in the center of the drink and at the last minute light the 151-proof rum on fire. Drink through straws without touching flame.

MARGARITA PARTY
Serves eight

3 cups tequila
2 cups Triple Sec
1½ cups lime cordial syrup
1¾ cups lime juice (fresh preferred)
1 cup cherry concentrate
Egg white
Salt
4 limes
½ pound fresh Montmorency cherries

Fill blender with ice, tequila, Triple Sec, lime cordial syrup, lime juice, cherry concentrate. Add dash egg white. Blend to desired consistency. Salt glass rims, fill glasses. Garnish with lime wedges and fresh cherries.

—Kelley Hebert

100

NORTHERN LIGHTS SANGRIA
Makes eight servings

1½ cups rum
½ cup sugar
1 thinly sliced orange
1 thinly sliced lemon
1 thinly sliced lime
1 cup frozen or fresh
     Montmorency cherries
1 bottle dry red wine
1 cup freshly squeezed orange juice
¼ cup cherry concentrate

Mix together rum and sugar in a large glass pitcher until sugar dissolves. Add fruit. Let sit for 2 to 6 hours in the refrigerator. Before serving, stir in wine, orange juice, cherry concentrate. Serve chilled. *Variation: Substitute white wine for red wine and vodka for rum for lighter-tasting sangria. Adjust cherry concentrate to taste.*
—Inspired by Annie and Roger Ducros

RUBY SLIPPERS
Serves twenty-five

12 lemons, juiced
6 limes, juiced
½ cup cherry concentrate
2 liters sparkling water
½ cup bar sugar
1 liter brandy
1 liter dry sherry
½ cup Triple Sec
½ cup cherry liqueur
2 oz. Kirschwasser
4 bottles champagne
½ pound fresh sweet cherries

Stir fruit juices, cherry concentrate, sparkling water and sugar in punch bowl. Add liquor and stir well. Add ice cubes. Float sweet cherries in punch bowl.

101

SCARLET SANGRIA
Makes eight servings

1 bottle red wine
2 cups ginger ale
¼ cup brandy
½ cup Triple Sec
4 slices orange
2 cups orange juice
¼ cup cherry concentrate

Mix together, and let sit in the refrigerator overnight.
The next day, pour over ice cubes and toss in a garnish
of fresh fruit.

BLEEDING HEART
Makes one shot

1 shot white crème de cacao
½ tsp. cherry concentrate

Coat shot glass with concentrate. Add crème de cacao.

CHERRY BOMB SHOT
Makes one shot

1 shot cherry brandy
Splash cinnamon schnapps

Shake, chill and strain as shot. Also great served on
the rocks.

—Jessica Corner, Big Eazy

CHERRY CHEESECAKE
Makes three to four shots

1½ oz. vanilla schnapps
1 oz. cherry juice
½ oz. cranberry juice
1 splash heavy cream

Add all ingredients to a shaker filled with ice. Shake
vigorously. Strain into shot glasses.

EIRE-CHERR

Makes one shot

1 shot Irish whiskey
1 tsp. cherry concentrate

Mix together.

FIRE & ICE

Makes one shot

1 shot vodka
1 dash cherry concentrate

Fill shot glass with vodka. Dip straw into cherry concentrate, trap concentrate inside straw, then gently release, swirling concentrate over vodka.

—Ronald Hoge

JAGERBOMBARDIER

Makes one drink

1 can Red Bull
1 Tbs. cherry concentrate
1 shot Jagermeister

Stir Red Bull, cherry together in pint glass. Fill shot glass with Jagermeister. Drop shot glass into pint glass.

LADY BRETT

Makes one shot

1 shot Cointreau
1 dash cherry juice (or concentrate)

Mix together.

NORTHERN GOTHIC

Makes one shot

1 shot cognac or brandy
½ tsp. cherry concentrate

Coat shot glass with concentrate. Add cognac.

103

CHOCOLATE-COVERED CHERRY JELL-O SHOTS
Makes one batch

3 oz. black cherry Jell-O
1 cup chilled cherry juice (Cairn Side
    recommended)
1 cup chilled vodka

Follow directions on Jell-O box, substituting cherry
juice and vodka for equal amount of cold water. Fill
small plastic shot glasses with mixture and chill overnight. Serve with chocolate whipped cream on top.
• *Variation: Jell-O can also be molded and cut into slices.*
—Sheila Paradis, Cairn Side Juice

PINEAPPLE JELL-O SHOTS
Makes one batch

3 oz. pineapple Jell-O
1 cup cherry juice
1 cup chilled vodka

Follow directions on Jell-O box, substituting cherry
juice and vodka for equal amount of cold water.
Fill small plastic shot glasses with mixture and chill
overnight • *Variation: Jell-O can also be molded and cut into
slices.*
—Tammi Elzinga

BRANDY HOT CHOCOLATE
Makes one drink

1 cup hot chocolate
1 oz. cherry brandy
Whipped cream
Chocolate syrup
1 cherry

Mix brandy into hot chocolate in mug. Top with
whipped cream, drizzle in chocolate. Garnish with
cherry.

FIERY BLUE BLAZER
Makes one cocktail

1 Tbs. honey
1 tsp. cherry concentrate
½ cup hot water
½ cup Scotch
Lemon twist
Dash of nutmeg

Dissolve honey, cherry concentrate in hot water. In a separate mug, ignite Scotch and pour mugs back and forth until the flame goes out. Pour into a heat-proof mug. Garnish with lemon twist, nutmeg.

•The Blue Blazer was created by bartender Jerry Thomas of New York City's Metropolitan Hotel in the 1800s. He considered it a tonic for cold weather and mixed it only when the thermometer read, at warmest, 10 degrees. Use extreme caution mixing flaming drinks.

HOT BUTTERED RUM
Makes many drinks

1 lb. brown sugar
½ lb. salted butter
1 tsp. nutmeg
1 tsp. cinnamon
1 tsp. cloves
1 tsp. cardamom
1 tsp. vanilla
1 mug very hot water
1 tsp. cherry concentrate
1 shot dark rum

To create batter, blend sugar, butter, nutmeg, cinnamon, cloves, cardamom, vanilla in food processor or blender, then store batter in freezer or refrigerator. To make a single drink, take 1-2 Tbs. of batter, stir into mug of very hot water. Stir in cherry concentrate. Add rum.

HOT HONEY & CHERRY
Makes one drink

1 oz. cherry concentrate
1 Tbs. honey (or more, to taste)
10 oz. hot water
1 shot whiskey

Mix together for a stiff warmer-upper. *Variation: Substitute spiced rum, or dark rum for whiskey.*

HOT MOCHA-CHERRY
Makes one drink

1 cup hot cocoa
1 shot Kahlua
1/2 shot cherry liqueur
Whipped cream
Chocolate syrup
1 cherry

Make hot cocoa. While still hot, stir in Kahlua and cherry liqueur. Top with whipped cream, a drizzle of chocolate syrup and garnish with cherry.

•Cherry concentrate may be added in lieu of liqueur. The drink is luxurious and rich but, because concentrate may separate from Kahlua and milk, it should be mixed well and consumed fairly quickly.

HOT TODDY
Makes one drink

¾ cup tea
1 Tbs. honey
2 shots brandy
1 lemon slice
1 tsp. cherry concentrate

Brew tea and fill a mug ¾ full. Stir in honey, then cherry concentrate, then brandy. Garnish with lemon slice.

MULLED CHERRY WINE
Makes four large portions

2 lemons
2 oranges
1 bottle cherry wine (Chateau Chantal
    recommended)
Nutmeg to taste
Cloves to taste
1 oz. cognac or Chateau Chantal Cerise
1 cup sugar
Herbal or citrus influenced tea (optional
    but excellent)
Water (optional softener instead of tea)
4 large cinnamon sticks

Cut lemons and oranges into slices. Pour the red wine into saucepan and gradually heat. Add fruit slices, nutmeg, cloves and cognac or Cerise. Keep an eye on the mixture and wait until it becomes hot to touch.

—Mark Johnson, Chateau Chantal

MULLED CIDER
Makes about one gallon

½ gallon apple cider
½ gallon cherry juice
¼ cup sugar
1 orange, halved, spiked with cloves
1 orange, sliced
2 cinnamon sticks
10-14 cloves
2 tsp. allspice
2½ cups dark rum

Mix cider, juice, sugar, oranges together in stock pot. Wrap up cinnamon, cloves, allspice in cheesecloth, tie shut and float in stockpot. Steep for 2-3 hours or more over low heat. Add rum 15 minutes before serving. Ladle or strain into mugs. *Variation: Instead of ½ gallon cherry juice, use ½ gallon cranberry plus ½ cup cherry concentrate.*

107

OLD SCHOOL
Makes one drink

1 oz. whiskey
1 mug near-boiling water
1 lemon slice, squeezed
1 tsp. honey
1 tsp. cherry concentrate

Mix all ingredients into water.

WARM GINGER KICK
Makes one drink

8 oz. ginger ale (Vernor's recommended)
1 tsp. cherry concentrate
1 shot spiced rum

Stir together and warm on stove or in microwave.

GLOSSARY

BALATON—America's newest tart, similar to the dark-skinned European Morello

BING—The dominant sweet is large, juicy, and mahogany-colored.

CERASELLA—A cherry liqueur made in Italy.

CHERISTOCK—A cherry liqueur made in Italy.

CHÉRI-SUISSE—A Swiss liqueur with a cherry-chocolate flavor.

CHERRY BRANDY—A liquor made from fermented cherry juice. Fruit brandes are called *eau de vie*. Mid-1990s changes in Michigan law allowed wineries to affordably produce distilled spirits. One bottle of cherry brandy may contain 30 pounds of cherries.

CERISE—A port-like cherry beverage produced by Chateau Chantal vineyard in Traverse City, Michigan. Cherry juice is fermented, then cherry brandy is added, which stops fermentation.

CHERRY CONCENTRATE—Until the mid-1990s, concentrate was sold in 55-gallon drums and used as flavoring in juice, gum and candy. Small firms then began repacking and selling it to consumers, initially to farm markets and health stores, later to some supermarkets. Small firms also are manufacturing 100 percent cherry juice now. Each ounce of concentrate contains about fifty cherries.

CHERRY HEERING— This Danish cherry liqueur was invented by Peter Heering and has been produced since 1818 without artificial ingredients from a top-secret family recipe. This sweet, dark-red liqueur became famous after the 1915 creation of the Singapore Sling.

CHERRY LIQUEUR— A sweet alcoholic beverage made from soaking or infusing cherries into spirits such as brandy, rum, whiskey or vodka. Many commercial liqueurs are made with closely guarded formulas. Cherries are among the best fruits with which to make homemade liqueur.

CHERRY MARNIER— A cherry liqueur made in France.

CRÈME DE CERISE—A French liqueur made with sweet cherries.

EARLY RICHMOND— A popular bright-red tart, the first spring cherry.

KIRSCH, KIRSHCHWASSER — A clear brandy distilled from cherry juice and pits. The name is German: kirsch ("cherry") and wasser ("water").

LAMBERT—A popular sweet cherry with rich flavor.

MARASCHINO CHERRY— Sweet Royal Ann cherries are pitted, bleached, soaked in almond- or mint-flavored sugar , then dyed red or green, to make maraschinos. The federal government banned harmful dyes that were used until recently.

MONTMORENCY — This dominant U.S. tart is used in pies, desserts, pastas, cereals, breads, meats.

MORELLO— A popular dark-skinned tart cherry.

RAINIER— A sweet variety with delicate taste and colorless juice.

ROYAL ANNE— A popular golden, red-blush sweet cherry.

SOUR CHERRIES— See tart cherries.

SWEET CHERRIES— There are more than 1,000 varieties of these firm, heart-shaped cherries, which can be eaten fresh or used in salads, sauces, desserts, breads. Best sellers are Bing, Lambert, Tartarian and Royal Ann

TART CHERRIES—Tarts are smaller, softer and more globular than sweets. Most are too tart to eat raw, but make excellent juice, pies and preserves. Best-selling varieties are Early Richmond, Montmorency and Morello.

TARTARIAN— A popular sweet cherry.

WISNIAK— A cherry liqueur made in Poland.

VAN—This late-season sweet cherry has a deep-red color.

CONTRIBUTORS

AMON ORCHARDS is a farm market in Acme, Michigan. *New York Times* writer R.W. Apple Jr. said it "sells the most luscious cherry jam I know."

RICHARD BEICHNER is executive chef at the Grand Traverse Resort and Spa in Acme, Michigan, where, from the 17th floor, you can see for miles and miles—all golf courses, Great Lakes and cherry orchards.

SANDRA BIAGINI lives in Northport, Michigan, and was the first person to contribute a recipe to this collection.

BILL BRIGGS is a retired school administrator who regularly enjoys a refreshing cherry spritzer to relieve aches and pains after a round of golf. He is the father of Karen Paradis, co-owner of Cairn Side Juice.

DEREK BROSSEAU is assistant manager of the Four Seasons Hotel in Washington, D.C. His Sake Cosmo toasts the 2003 Cherry Blossom Festival.

JESSICA CORNER is a bartender at the Big Eazy Fish Haus and Blues Company in Traverse City, Michigan.

CHERRY MARKETING INSTITUTE, based in Lansing, Michigan, is a national research and promotion group that represents U.S. tart cherry growers.

STEVE DETAR is owner of Brownwood Acres Foods, a family-owned business that produces organic products. It's located in Eastport, Michigan.

MELANIE DRANE is a poet who teaches creative writing at the Interlochen Arts Academy in Interlochen, Michigan. She is a winner of a MacArthur fellowship and the Morris Croll Poetry Prize from Princeton. She's also a former wine/food columnist for the *Daily Yomiuri* and *Japan Times* in Tokyo. Her Wild Cherry Lifesaver Martini is "so yummy, it's dangerous."

ANNIE AND ROGER DUCROS live on France's Cotes d'Azur but make it up to the Cherry Capital—home of their "American Family"—as often as possible. They suggest that the proper spelling of cherries is *cerise*.

EDEN FOODS is an organic food manufacturer that began as a co-op in 1968 in Ann Arbor, Michigan.

CHRIS EDSON is owner of Edson Farms, a happy-spirited family-owned natural foods store in Traverse City, Michigan.

TAMMI ELZINGA enthusiastically thinks of such perfect touches as freezing cherries in ice cubes and dripping concentrate inside glasses for Halloween scariness. She lives in Traverse City, Michigan, with her husband, Greg, and daughter, Paige.

RAYMELL ENGLISH goes for glam with precise aim: Creating gorgeous sugar-rimmed champagne drinks for these pages, among other inventions. This grown-up princess is a family specialist who lives in Traverse City, Michigan, with her son, Micajah Zajic.

DANIEL H. GORNEY is a photographer whose work has appeared in *Newsweek*, the *Detroit Free Press*, and other publications, and who doubles as an exceptional bartender.

SHANNON HALL works with Alzheimer's patients, owns Clean Start cleaning company, and is grandmother to Zoe and Jack. She's also a painter of poppies. She lives in Traverse City, Michigan.

TIMOTHY HALL is a graphic designer, director of the indie movie *Vow*, and owner of Tempest Cinematique, a film production company in Traverse City, Michigan. His Miss American Pie recipe, inspired by "good ol' boys drinking whiskey and rye," was the last of the late-breaking drinks allowed into these pages.

ZOE MILAGRO HALL is a joy. She's the daughter of Kristyn Houle and Timothy Hall, and she is the youngest contributor to this book.

KELLEY HEBERT is a Royal Canadian Mounted Police Officer who was last spotted in Saskatchewan, Canada. Previously, she played Julie Your Cruise Director on such liners as the Regent Rainbow, out of Florida.

RONALD HOGE is a world traveler and devoted drinker. He named many, many cocktails in this collection.

BILLY HOXIE is an artist in Traverse City, Michigan, who came up with his Fire Engine recipe on the spot, upon demand.

ROBERT HUGHES, an animator who lives in Traverse City, Michigan, spent childhood summers on Lake Michigan's South Manitou Island, where jars of cherry bounce under the bed were an ongoing curiosity. Rob still thinks Aunt Toy made the bounce, when really it was Aunt Polly.

JUDY FRISKE KEHR is with Friske's Farm Market near Charlevoix, Michigan. The Friskes are pioneers in marketing frozen (IQF) cherries.

MARK JOHNSON is a winemaker at Chateau Chantal on Old Mission Peninsula, Michigan, and was among winemakers who visited Germany in 1998 to learn about making *eau de vie*, or fruit brandy, after Michigan relaxed distillation regulations.

BRAD KLIMASZEWSKI is a bartender at Amical, a restaurant in downtown Traverse City, Michigan, with a stellar menu, cozy fireplace and a patio where beautiful people have been known to sit all day drinking Bellinis.

BRUCE LIABLE is a bartender at Big Eazy Fish Haus and Blues Company in Traverse City, Michigan.

JOYCE LALONDE is a lifelong educator and political activist. Her Cherry Cosmopolitan has been tasted from Michigan to Washington, D.C.

LEELANAU FRUIT COMPANY is located in Suttons Bay, Michigan.

SUSAN LITTLEFIELD-DUNGJEN is a schoolteacher, amazing vocalist and accomplished thespian who lives in Cedar, Michigan, with husband Bill, son Jeremiah, and dog Dart(agnon).

MACKINAW BREWING COMPANY is a restaurant in downtown Traverse City, Michigan, and is possibly located at the geographic heart of the National Cherry Festival's Cherry Royale Parade route.

NANCY MCINTOSH lives in Ohio, though she returns to her dad's orchard, McIntosh Orchards, near Mount Pleasant, Michigan, to help keep it in production. She has many memories of picking, sorting and selling sweet and sour cherries each summer while growing up.

LEIGH MCKOLAY is a bartender at the Beacon Lounge in Traverse City, Michigan, whose liquor-bottle xylophoning is unrivaled.

NABIEL MUSLEH is manager of Minerva's restaurant and the Beacon Lounge in Traverse City, Michigan.

MAT AND LEAH NICHOLSON are northern Michigan natives who form the entire graphic design department of Cairn Side Juice, owned by their cousin Tom. The inspiration for their recipes came from the juice itself.

NORTH PEAK BREWING COMPANY is a restaurant and microbrewery in Traverse City, Michigan. Theirs is the only recipe calling for a keg.

DONNA PARADIS owns and operates Eastport Village Care Home, where all of the residents regularly enjoy drinking Cairn Side Cherry Juice.

SANDRA PARADIS and her husband, Glenn, own and operate Northwind Farms, growing cherries, apples, and other fruit. Glenn's father, Mitchell Paradis, owned the original Cairn Side Farms. Sandra, who recently retired from Mill Creek Schools, enjoys not only the great taste, but also the fizz and color of her festive Pink Cherry Blossom.

SHEILA PARADIS and her husband, Mike, own and operate Nik-Col Farms, growing cherries, apples and other fruit. Mike's father Mitchell owned the original Cairn Side Farms. Sheila developed her Chocolate-Covered Cherry Jell-O Shot recipe as a way to combine two of her favorite tastes: chocolate and cherries.

TOM AND KAREN PARADIS own Cairn Side Farms in Kewadin, Michigan. Tom is a third-generation cherry farmer who, with his grandpa Mitchell Paradis, developed Cairn Side's Norwegian Saft Cooking method for making pure juice from homegrown Grade-A cherries. All recipes were developed at one of many family happy hours.

AUSTIN PHAM is a bartender at the Garden Terrace Lounge in the Four Seasons Hotel, Washington, D.C. His Sake Cosmo is a fine example of what an inside-the-beltway pro can do with real cherry juice.

BECKY PIAZZA owns Miller's Family Orchard in Vassar, Michigan. Her cherry cordial is one of several generations-old farm recipes.

RAY "MR. CHERRY USA" PLEVA is a former butcher who, with his daughter, then the reigning National Cherry Festival queen, came up with a cherry-enhanced sausage. Customers said they felt so much better after eating it that Pleva began championing research, which ultimately led to the discovery of antioxidants in cherries. Pleva has since appeared on *Oprah*. He now sells his products to schools and the military, has operations in Japan and continues to crusade for cherry research—most notably feeding a steer named Buzz cherries, then shipping his brain to researchers.

SHAWN "BIG DADDY" ROBINSON is bar manager of The Big Eazy Fish Haus and Blues Company in Traverse City, Michigan.

MARY A. SMITH is a chemist, home economist and the owner of Smith Orchards in Omena, who's patented a cherry flavor enhancer and conducts work to find new uses of cherries, including pastes. She was among a group of well-connected Leelanau County, Michigan, Rotarians who pitched cherries to major U.S. corporations.

SHERWOOD SMITH is a vice president with The Intelligence Agency, a marketing firm, and the founder of Arthur's Natural Foods. He lives in Traverse City, Michigan, with wife, architect Suzannah Tobin, and sons, Arthur and Elliot. He is a good neighbor.

RICHARD STEARNS owns Sunrise Dried Fruit in Northport, Michigan.

JACKSON STEELE loves fire trucks. He is the son of Lori Hall Steele and Brian Steele, and is this book's second-youngest contributor.

TERESA SULLIVAN is an avid celebrator and has the distinction of submitting the only recipe that needs to be shaken long enough for ice crystals to form. She is director of Pituitary Disorders Education & Support in Brighton, Michigan, and is mother to Alia and Megan.

BOB SUTHERLAND is owner of Cherry Republic, a gleeful cheerleader of all things cherry in Glen Arbor, Michigan, where the slogan is "Life, Liberty, Beaches & Pie."

MATT AND VICTORIA SUTHERLAND throw some fine cocktail parties in Traverse City, Michigan. Victoria is publisher of *Foreword* magazine, and Matt is a writer, editor and brother of Cherry Republic's Bob Sutherland.

HERB AND MARY TEICHMAN own Tree-Mendus Fruit Inc. in Eau Claire, Michigan, home of the International Cherry Pit Spit each summer.

PAULETTE TILKINGTON is with Brownwood Acres in Eastport, Michigan.

MICHAEL TRUBAC is with TraVino Traverse Wine and Grille in Acme, Michigan.

TERRY VANKLEEK homeschools his children in Traverse City, Michigan. His Fireball cocktail—with tequila, cherry and Tabasco—remains untested. Hopefully this is understandable.

JOHN VIDERGAR, vice president of Leland Cherry Company, is committed to the cherry industry. His Cherry Bomb has spread throughout Leelanau County, Michigan.

MARY WALLER is vice president of Brownwood Acres in Eastport, Michigan.

MICHELLE WHITE, president of Leland Cherry Company in Leland, Michigan, is dedicated to the preservation of farmland and specializes in cherry promotion. She continuously comes up with new cherry-usage ideas, like her famous cherry margarita.

INDEX

Names of cherry drink recipes contained in this book appear in uppercase.

119

ACKNOWLEDGMENTS

I'd like to thank each contributor for their creativity and for help-ing expose people to cherry drinks. I'd also like to thank Dr. Russel Reiter, Ph.D., of the University of Texas Health Science Center, author of *Melatonin,* for writing the foreword to this book.

I owe many drinks to Dr. James M. Schaefer, Ph.D., a leading international expert in the use of alcohol. He has conducted studies for the National Institutes of Health, among others, and generously shepherded and interpreted this book's double-blind study on whether cherries diminish hangovers. His expertise was priceless. Thanks, too, to all nineteen of the study's subjects, some of whom unfortunately did suffer on the behalf of science. I'd also like to thank Raymell English and Tammi Elzinga for help with the tests.

Very special thanks to the team that assisted with production in large and small ways. Book packager Mary Jo Zazueta, owner of To The Point Solutions, provided enthusiastic direction, impeccable technical assistance, and copyediting. Daniel H. Gorney shot the author photo, and Barbara Henry shot the cover photo. Eric Gustafson designed and programmed Web sites. And writer and editor Anne Stanton, who authored *Publish to Win: Smart Strategies to Sell More Books,* proofed pages and helped me keep the faith. I'd like to thank Ronald Hoge for his ingenuity with drink names.

To Alex Moore, Melanie Drane, Tom Carr and Diane Conners —thank you for writerly insight, professional wisdom and support. Special thanks, too, to Rob Hughes, Jerry Johnson, Jim Moore, Blake Ringsmuth, Ivan Pylypchuk, Sarah and Junior Saluta, Megan Welch and Sara Winterman. I'd like to thank the farmers and agricultural experts I've interviewed over the years for various cherry-related newspaper and magazine articles, particularly Jane Baker DePriest at the Cherry Marketing Institute in Lansing, Michigan.

Special thanks to my mother, Shannon Hall, who not only always serves drinks in the good glasses but also believes strongly in toasting to everything, because it matters. She stayed up stuffing envelopes, babysat and helped set up the drink tests. Very special thanks to my brother, Timothy Hall, a graphic designer and filmmaker, for being there. He provided invaluable technical support with design, and gave me—and others—sheer inspiration for Just Doing It when he premiered his independent film *Vow* in 2003. I'd like to thank Kristyn Houle for dreaming up cherry slogans. Literally. Thanks too, to my brother, David Hall, and sister, Teresa Sullivan, for enduring support; and to my sister, Marci, for all the halcyon moments when our glasses clinked.

Finally, I'd like to thank my son, Jackson Gabriel, who loves to toast with his sippy cup, and who tried hard to nap, even after discovering he couldn't sleep when it's daytime.

ABOUT THE AUTHOR

Lori Hall Steele is a writer and editor. She is a recipient of a Robert F. Kennedy Journalism Award and her book copyediting credits include the bestseller *Dude, Where's My Country?* She studied journalism at the University of London and received her bachelor's from Michigan State University, before settling just blocks from the bluest Great Lake. She lives in the nation's Cherry Capital—Traverse City, Michigan—with her young son, Jackson, and only began drinking cherry juice for professional reasons. Turns out, she liked it.